If This Is Love,
Why Am I Unhappy?

The 3 Keys To Having
The Relationship You Want

SCOTT KUDIA, PH.D.

ISBN 0-7414-3328-1

Published by:

PUBLISHING.COM

1094 New DeHaven Street, Suite 100
West Conshohocken, PA 19428-2713
Info@buybooksontheweb.com
www.buybooksontheweb.com
Toll-free (877) BUY BOOK
Local Phone (610) 941-9999
Fax (610) 941-9959

Printed in the United States of America

Printed on Recycled Paper

Published February 2008

CONTENTS

For Lindsay, you fill my heart with laughter and love
To Bobbi, for your generous time and energy
To Lori, my dear friend and champion

Warning - Disclaimer

The Cinderella Syndrome

"If love is the answer,
could you rephrase the question?"
LILY TOMLIN

What's the difference between people who are happy in their relationships and people who are not? Is it intelligence? It can't be. We all know plenty of stupid people who have better relationships than we do. Is it beauty? No. We all know plenty of less attractive people who are happier than we are in their relationships. Is it money? No way. There are plenty of people who are poorer than we are that are more satisfied with their relationships. So what is the difference between people who are happy and those who are unhappy with their relationships? The answer to that question is the subject of this book.

It's pretty simple, really. The quality of our relationships depends on three things: what we think, what we feel, and what we do. These are the three keys to getting more out of your relationship. If you change all three of these you will experience a dramatic improvement in your relationship.

***When you stop making a contribution to your
relationship the relationship begins to die.***

WHAT IS LOVE?

For centuries, poets, authors, songwriters, and Hollywood
films have told us that everything about love should feel like
weak knees and sweaty palms. We get buried under a
barrage of myths like, "love at first sight" or "I'm nothing
without you" or "happily ever after." These ideals lead us to
believe love just happens and when it does it solves all our
problems. We say "I do" and we're done. Our expectations
are set according to the fairy tales, poems, romance novels,
love songs, and movies we've seen and we're always
disappointed when we realize the truth. Loving relationships
don't just happen. They take time, energy, patience, respect,
cooperation, and commitment. That doesn't sound very
exciting or romantic, does it? It can if you want it to be. The
fact is when you stop making a contribution to your
relationship the relationship begins to die.

*"It is not for the love of a husband that a husband is
dear; but for the love of the Soul of the husband that
a husband is dear. It is not for the love of a wife that
a wife is dear; but for the love of the Soul of the wife
that a wife is dear."*

THE UPANISHADS

We want to believe true love is what's portrayed in the
movies because we want it to be more than what our parents
showed us. We hope and pray loving relationships are not
really as mundane as what we saw from our parents'
marriage. Such unrealistic expectations set us up for huge
disappointment. It is next to impossible to feel those
butterflies in your stomach every day for thirty or forty

years. Because love is a process, the butterflies eventually fly away and a deeper level of commitment and companionship takes over. Problems may arise if the partners begin to take each other for granted, or worse, they begin to play out their childhood disappointments. Love stories don't tell us that part.

Fairy tales don't show us what happens after the guy gets the girl. They don't tell us what happens after Cinderella marries Prince Charming. We don't see how she eventually resents his Friday nights out with the guys while she's at home watching the kids. They don't show us how he resents her for being too controlling and demanding. Most of us would be shocked to see Cinderella constantly yearning to be romanced and swept off her feet again just like Charming did in the beginning of the relationship. Instead, Cinderella is left feeling frustrated and lonely in their seven-bedroom castle.

We are only shown the exciting part of the relationship like the flirting, the romance, the envious onlookers, and that blissful first kiss. What we don't get to see are the arguments and power struggles, the resentment and frustration. The story ends before Cinderella yells at Charming to load the dishwasher the "right" way as he ignores her and continues watching the game. We especially don't get to see how the abuse Cinderella suffered at the hands of her stepmother and stepsisters causes her to verbally abuse and control Charming. We're never aware of the tears she cries because her relationship isn't what the Fairy Godmother promised. The frustration she feels from not knowing what's wrong with the relationship or how to fix it remains untold as well.

The fact is Cinderella has a bit of work to do on herself before her relationship will improve. And it will improve. By learning how what she saw, heard, and experienced growing up is running her relationship today, she will be able to change what she thinks, how she feels, and the way she behaves. When she does she will be able to get more from her relationship. While it's true that Charming may be a bit of a passive or lazy partner, it's also true that she chooses to stay with him. So there must be a reason she remains despite the frustration and disappointment.

It's more than simply loving him. Cinderella is receiving some sort of emotional benefit by controlling Charming. Once she acknowledges this, she will be able to change her controlling tendencies and use more appropriate behavior to meet her needs. When she decides to make some changes in how she thinks, feels, and behaves, he'll have to change, as well. If he doesn't, she'll find someone who's better suited for her.

> *"I love being married. It's so great to find that one special person you want to annoy for the rest of your life."*
> RITA RUDNER

WHEN CUTE BECOMES ANNOYING

Because of unrealistic expectations, most people think that all they need is love to make a relationship work. The problem is they don't hang around long enough for love to develop. They get high on the physical chemistry, excitement, and freshness that come from getting to know someone new and they interpret that as being in love. When these "symptoms" begin to wear off they think they must not really love that person and they begin looking for their next "true love."

We are led to believe that we should continuously feel butterflies in our stomach just as we did in the early months of dating. But when the butterflies fly south for the winter we panic and think we must not be in love any more. His cute little idiosyncrasies suddenly become annoying bad habits that drive us crazy. When the butterflies are gone we look for reasons why. "It must be because he eats his peas one at a time" or "She takes forever getting ready" or "He never says please." We think, "If I don't have butterflies, if I no longer get weak in the knees, then I must not love him as much as I thought. And one of the reasons I must not love him as much is because he eats his damn peas one at a time." But he ate his peas one at time on the first date and it didn't bother you then. Why is it suddenly bothering you now? But bother you it does.

More and more, we grow to hate his "annoying" habits. These habits and our feelings about them become linked. Once they get linked it becomes self-perpetuating and creates a vicious cycle. The more we notice the habit the more irritated we become. The more irritated we are, the more we hate the habit. We believe that if the sweaty palms and butterflies are gone, we should start looking at his faults as reasons why. It's funny how we overlook our own shortcomings in the process, isn't it?

"We sleep in separate rooms, we have dinner apart, we take separate vacations, we're doing everything we can to keep our marriage together."

RODNEY DANGERFIELD

In our fantasies we see what our ideal mate looks like, what it's like to be around him, and how it feels to be continuously happy, excited, and sexually passionate for him. But no one can live up to a fantasy. Nevertheless, we are not ready to accept that we won't feel that constant love buzz forever. Instead we are dismayed when we feel annoyed, tired, bored, or emotionally distant. We don't want to admit that the relationship will include bad breath, disappointment, dirty underwear, or snoring.

THE GRASS IS GREENER OVER THERE

As human beings we are never satisfied. We tend to take for granted and get bored with the things and people in our life. When this happens we believe our happiness is just on the other side of our hum drum daily existence. When we get comfortable with a new car or a new relationship we begin to compare it to everything and everyone else. This comparison, this "grass is always greener" way of thinking, is what causes our dissatisfaction with what we currently have.

Conflict and issues that arise during the course of the relationship are other areas that cause us to pause from our adoration. We're brought up thinking if we meet our soul mate we won't have anything to argue about because we're made for each other. When conflict does arise, we panic and think he's not "the one." We fail to understand that conflict is necessary to all relationships. It's how a relationship is able to grow and evolve.

When a broken bone heals, the area over the break calcifies. This calcification makes that part of the bone stronger than it was before the break. Working through and resolving conflict in relationships makes the relationship stronger than it was before the disagreement. Resolving issues takes honesty, respect, trust, and clear communication; all of which strengthen the relationship and help it to evolve. In fact, research suggests that conflict and its healthy resolution are crucial to the development of a respectful, loving relationship. Couples who rarely argue may be avoiding conflict, which means they are likely suppressing opinions and feelings and harboring resentment or contempt.

Working through and resolving conflict makes the relationship stronger than it was before.

Another reason we can't be happy or blissful all the time is that frustration is an inherent part of living and completely unavoidable. When our emotional, physical, spiritual, or sexual needs are met we immediately want more. This wanting more is what causes frustration and drives most of us crazy. It is impossible to be positive and cheerful all the time. I'll bet that's a relief for those of you who thought this was just another "positive thinking" book.

When you're using dial-up to surf the Internet you may be very pleased to have the world at your fingertips. But, when you switch from dial-up to high-speed Internet, you may suddenly realize how painfully slow dial-up was. The same thing happens with Sore Spots. We've lived with the Sore Spot for so long that we don't realize how much it's slowing us down. It's so ingrained as a habit that you may not even know how you're contributing to the problem. When you heal your Sore Spot you will discover how Destructive the old behavior was.

"If you continue to do what you have always done, you will continue to get what you have always gotten."

PROVERB

As human beings we always want more. A second helping at dinner, two scoops of ice cream instead of one, 800 instead of 500 channels to choose from, more money, more time, and especially more love. The human mind operates by comparison. It compares what it has to what it used to have. It gets a little more of something and then compares it to what it had before.

Some people think marriage is the answer to all their problems. Since well over half of all marriages end in divorce, it's pretty obvious those people are wrong. Marriage doesn't solve any problems. If anything, it exposes and worsens issues they've ignored, denied, or failed to resolve. You have to have a strong relationship foundation in order to give marriage a fighting chance.

"Women marry men hoping they will change. They don't. Men marry women hoping they won't change. They do."

BETTINA ARNDT

Nowadays we get caught up with reality TV shows like The Bachelor, which try to convince us that simply being picked out of a crowd constitutes true love and will make us eternally happy. This message gets pummeled into our senses. But the message is wrong.

Still others try to turn sex into a relationship. They mistake great sex for true love. But sex is sex. It does not equal love. You can have sex with someone and not be in love or even like the person. Some people think since the sex is good the rest will follow. The problem is, while sex is an important part of a relationship, its not the most important. Couples who don't take the time to establish a strong foundation soon discover how shallow the relationship is because it's based solely on sex.

"Love is the best gift you can give. It gives more pleasure to the giver than to the receiver."

M.K. SONI

SOWING THE SEEDS OF LOVE

Love is a process. There is no such thing as love at first sight. It takes time to develop and grow. It takes commitment, trust, effective communication, honesty,

8

respect, and compassion. These seeds are planted early in the relationship and don't even begin to blossom until months, and in most cases years later. In order for love to bloom, you need to take care of the seeds you've planted.

If you plant a seed but never water it, it won't grow. You must water the seed and nurture the plant. When it gets bigger you have to change the pot and continue fertilizing and watering it. If you don't change the pot it will stop growing. Relationships act much like the seed. They need love, attention, and room to grow. If you don't change the pot, the relationship won't grow. Soon you both feel trapped and frustrated. Changing the pot means working through your issues so the relationship can evolve.

"Love is like a beautiful flower, which I may not touch but whose fragrance makes the garden a place of delight just the same."

HELEN KELLER

I'm not talking about the "what color should we paint the living room" or "should we get a dog" problems. I'm talking about the big issues that undermine trust and commitment and stop relationships in their tracks. I'm talking about the issues that keep coming up again and again in every one of our relationships or in the same relationship. Controlling our partners, becoming passive during conflicts, throwing tantrums, and fearing intimacy. Now these are real issues that cut right to the heart of the relationship.

Most people ignore these problems and think if they just make a few changes they'll be all right. So they change their hair, change their cars, change their jobs, change their wardrobe, they even change partners. Then they think, "Okay, now I'm ready for a great relationship." If that was all it took we'd all have the perfect partner and we'd all have a perfect relationship.

But all those things are outside of us. Those who are willing to look inside themselves, people like you, simply refuse to settle any more. I know. I've been there, too. Like me, you decided it's time to do whatever it takes to get more from your relationship. Something inside you is saying, "No more rotten relationships. I don't want to be lonely. I don't want to be embarrassed about how I behave in my relationship. I don't want to be with someone who's not right for me anymore. I've wasted enough time."

Love is a process.

I would have the same issues pop up over and over again in my relationships. I kept thinking if only she'd do this or if only she didn't do that, then I'd be happy. It didn't matter who I was dating. It would be a different name but the same old problem. It wasn't until I stopped and looked at myself that I discovered a Destructive pattern in my relationships, or what I call a Sore Spot. The same pattern kept repeating over and over in my relationships. That's why I dated the same kind of women and acted the same way in each of my relationships.

I discovered that what I learned as a child is what I carried over into my adult relationships. This blew me away because I hadn't really thought about how what I saw as a child would cause me to make specific decisions as an adult. You were a child once, too, and what you learned from childhood is running your relationships today.

If what you learned was love, respect, commitment, and trust, then you are probably satisfied with your relationship. The majority of us, however, didn't learn these qualities. The result is one or more Sore Spots that keep us from having the

10

relationship we've dreamed of since we first played "house" as a child.

It's almost embarrassing to admit how many times I unwittingly stopped my relationships dead in their tracks because what I was thinking and doing was sabotaging it. And the only thing that separates you and me is that I've done the work already. That's why I'm sharing it with you. I know once you're reminded of what you already know deep down inside you will be in control of the quality of your relationship. Since you've read this far that means you're looking for a way to get more from your relationship. You are in search of a way to get your relationship to be the way it used to be or to be the way you always dreamed it would be.

"Don't be afraid to go out on a limb.
That's where the fruit is."

H. JACKSON BROWNE

GETTING STARTED

So, how do we do this? I wrote this book to empower, educate, and support you through your change work. The more you understand about how a Sore Spot is created and why it keeps happening, the easier it is for you to eliminate that Sore Spot and the easier it is to create the quality of relationship you want. So, you will discover how your thoughts and beliefs about yourself, your partner, and your relationships determine the quality of your relationships. We'll examine what our greatest needs are in our relationships. We'll also look at what scares us the most and how that fear can sabotage and destroy a perfectly good relationship.

Next, you'll be shown examples of Sore Spots and their causes, including the importance of healthy self-esteem in our relationships. Finally, we'll unravel the mystery of the role our parents played and still play in our current relationships. Once you understand how a Sore Spot is created and why it keeps hurting your relationship, you'll get to the root cause and stop it from happening again. Together we'll identify, understand, and eliminate your Sore Spot. Use this program for as many Sore Spots as you are aware. I still use this program to clear new issues and Sore Spots that periodically appear.

Focus on raising the quality of your relationship instead of trying to make it perfect.

Pop psychologists preach to us about having a perfect relationship. But "perfect" is different for everybody. So what I'd like you to do as you read these pages is focus on raising the *quality* of your relationship rather than striving for perfection. Perfection is elusive, while raising the quality is attainable. Having more of something you want is easier than making it perfect. So, focus on getting *more* of what you want from your relationship.

THE FLOOD

There is a story of a religious man who lived alone. A tremendous storm was bringing torrential rains and the town began to flood. The man immediately began to pray for help and guidance from God. Suddenly he was interrupted by a knock at the door. When the man opened the door he saw his two good friends standing there. They urged him to come with them to find safe refuge. The man declined saying God would take care of him.

When the water was up to his kitchen table the man began to panic a bit and so he prayed even harder for assistance from God. As the water continued to rise he opened his window and saw a boat outside. A man inside the boat urged him to come with him to a safe place. Again the man refused saying he didn't need assistance because God would help him.

When the floodwaters were up to the roof of his house, the man stood on the top of his roof, praying even harder for God to help him. Just then, a helicopter flew overhead and dropped a ladder down to the man. Again the man refused to climb aboard because he said God would help him.

Eventually the floodwaters became so deep and turbulent that the man could struggle no longer and he drowned. On his journey to the after life the man found himself face to face with God. "Why didn't you help me?" asked the man, "Why didn't you answer my prayers?" God looked at the man with love and compassion and said, "I sent your two friends to get you, I sent the boat, and I sent you a helicopter. What more do you want from me?"

> *"It wasn't raining when Noah built the Ark."*
>
> HOWARD RUFF

The point is I will guide you to where you need to be in order to let go of what's troubling your relationship. You still have to do the work. I can't do it for you. Just making the decision to change doesn't make it happen. You must act on what you've learned. Making the decision to get something that hurts out of your eye is a lot different than actually doing it. So we're going to do it. We're going to get what's painful out of your relationship. I promise you when you do, you'll learn more about yourself than ever before and it will change the way you experience your relationship.

> *"Knowledge is only potential power."*
>
> NAPOLEON HILL

Often times the signs are all there but we don't see them because we've lived with the Sore Spot for so long it's become "normal" for us. In most cases it's been with us since childhood.

The things we learned as children influence the degree to which we are satisfied with our current love life. Most recurring problems in our relationships can be traced back to the emotional disappointments suffered in childhood. These childhood hurts create Sore Spots in our adult relationships. As long as we are unaware of these Sore Spots and their causes our frustration will continue to grow. It is only by uncovering the root cause of the Sore Spot that we are able to see how it is sabotaging our relationship and stop any further damage.

2

What Lurks
Beneath The Surface

*"In order for us to reach success
we must first find the ladder."*

ROBERT M. HENSEL

Termites eat away at the foundation of a house without really being noticed. It's only when the house starts to fall apart, after the damage is done, that we notice the problem. The fact is most relationships don't end due to one large conflict. Instead, most people let recurring problems sabotage the relationship over time. These chronic issues are Sore Spots. So, let's define Sore Spot.

SORE SPOTS

A Sore Spot is something that keeps coming up over and over again in every relationship or in the same relationship again and again. A Sore Spot is something you do that you know harms the relationship but for some reason you just can't stop doing it. For example, maybe you start arguments too often, or perhaps you just can't let anyone get close to you, or you pout until you get your way. What's interesting about Sore Spots is we often think we behave this way because of something our partner either is or is not doing. The reality is the Sore Spot is connected to what you learned from your parents as a child and only you can do anything about it.

Furthermore, whatever the Sore Spot is, it's only a symptom of what's really going on. If we treat a symptom are we treating the cause? No. If I get a cat and suddenly start sneezing and then find out I'm allergic to cats, should I treat the sneeze? That's treating the symptom. You need to treat the cause. In this case cat dander. You have to remove the cat. The cat is the root cause of the sneezing. Remove the cat and the sneezing stops.

You don't just fix the wood. You get rid of what's damaging the wood. You get rid of the termites. One termite taking a bite is no big deal. But that same termite taking a bite again and again in the same spot will weaken and eventually destroy the foundation.

If you looked at the same event through the eyes of a non-frustrated person you wouldn't be frustrated either.

If you're frustrated, the frustration is a symptom of what's really going on. You must determine why you allow yourself to be frustrated. Notice I didn't say determine *what's* frustrating you. I said you must determine why you *allow yourself* to be frustrated. What's frustrating you is outside of you and outside of your control. Why you allow yourself to be frustrated is inside of you and completely within your control. The same situation may not frustrate someone else. This is how we know the frustration is coming from inside us. If you looked at the same event through the eyes of the non-frustrated person you wouldn't be frustrated either.

If you are abused, the abuse is a symptom. You must determine why you allow yourself to be abused. If you're angry, why do you allow yourself to be angered? If you're passive, what is it inside you that allows you to let people walk all over you? The answer can be found in our thoughts. What we think determines whether or not we will be angry, sad, passive, or frustrated. Everything, good or bad, begins with a thought. So, why do we have these thoughts and how do we go about changing them? The chapters that follow will answer these questions and more. First, let's discover how to recognize a Sore Spot.

LOOKING FOR CLUES

There are four clues to look for that determines whether or not it's a Sore Spot.

Clue #1: **It keeps happening.** Whether it's a series of relationships or a single long-term relationship, the same issue keeps popping up again and again. For instance, you may continually date all the wrong guys or throw tantrums every time you feel neglected.

Clue #2: **It only gives short-term gratification.** There is no long-term benefit. It only provides temporary relief and doesn't solve the problem. For instance, you explode out of frustration and feel better in the moment, but it doesn't do anything to solve why you're frustrated or prevent the frustration in the future.

Clue #3: **It has Destructive side effects for you and others.** It's not good for you, your partner, or the relationship. Yelling at your partner doesn't solve the problem and you lose his respect and trust while generating more resentment each time you explode.

Clue #4: You feel bad when it appears. It makes you feel bad or maybe worse than you did before. It may be a relief to explode when you're frustrated, but in the long run you'll both harbor resentment for each other. Resentment destroys a relationship from the inside out.

The trickiest clue is that last one. It's tricky because sometimes we're not aware we feel bad. We often rationalize or justify our outbursts saying he did something to make you act that way. We think to ourselves, "If he'd put the damn toilet seat down I wouldn't have to yell at him." Think about it. Our irritations come from a perceived refusal to conform to the way we think things should be. Who decides the way things should be? Is your way better than his just because it's your way? Is it more important to have things done your way while resentment eats away at your relationship, or would a cooperative, respectful, and loving relationship be better?

Our irritations come from a perceived refusal to conform to the way we think things should be.

Sore Spots are open wounds. We may think everything's okay because it's scabbed over. But eventually it will be ripped off and it'll hurt more than it did the last time. We're not putting a band-aid over it anymore. We're cleaning it out and letting it heal. When we heal something, whether it's physical, emotional, or spiritual, it returns to a state of wholeness. It may hurt in the beginning when it's getting cleaned out but as it begins to heal and you become whole again, you will notice remarkable changes in your relationship.

Here is a list of some of the Sore Spots I've helped my clients eliminate. Do you see any that are familiar to you? If you see more than one, rest assured you're not alone. You can use this program to let go of as many as you uncover.

- I get angry every time _____.
- I get frustrated whenever _____.
- I get sad or depressed when _____.
- I deny what's really happening when _____.
- I withdraw, pout, or give the silent treatment when _____.
- I stop listening when _____.
- I get jealous whenever _____.
- I intentionally hurt him when _____.
- I get afraid whenever _____.
- I feel guilty whenever _____.
- I try to change or "fix" him by _____.
- I put myself down whenever _____.
- I "mother" my partner by _____.
- I "chase after love" or try to "earn" his love and approval by _____.
- I resent it whenever _____.
- I feel hurt whenever _____.
- I get defensive whenever _____.
- I feel lonely when _____.
- I blame, accuse, or find fault with my boyfriend whenever _____.
- I cheat or have affairs whenever _____.
- I intentionally sabotage the relationship when _____.
- I become controlling whenever _____.
- I lose control every time _____.

- I reject him whenever _____.
- I lie or "forget" to tell certain things when _____.
- I neglect him every time _____.
- I get shy whenever _____.
- I break down and cry whenever _____.
- I overreact every time _____.
- I explode whenever _____.
- I pass the buck on responsibility when _____.
- I feel insecure whenever _____.
- I go from relationship to relationship or can't be alone.
- I don't feel worthy or good enough.
- I take him back when he cheats.
- I think, "Screw you! I don't need anyone. I'm better off alone."
- I pick all the wrong guys.
- I'm afraid he'll leave me/fear of abandonment.
- I fear commitment.

"When written in Chinese, the word 'crisis' is composed of two characters…one represents danger, and the other represents opportunity."

JOHN F. KENNEDY

WHICH SCREW DO I TURN?

A business owner was in a panic. His assembly line had suddenly stopped and he was losing a million dollars an hour. Needless to say, he was overjoyed when the repairman showed up. The owner watched anxiously as the repairman looked at the machine for a couple minutes, then pulled a screwdriver from his toolbox and turned a screw one-quarter of a turn. The assembly line started up as suddenly as it had stopped. The owner was elated. He thanked the repairman and asked how much he owed. The repairman stated the fee for fixing the assembly line was $1000.00. The infuriated business owner screamed, "This is outrageous! It's ridiculous! You didn't even do anything. You turned a screw. I demand you give me an itemized bill and I'm not paying you one cent until you do." Upon hearing this, the repairman pulled out a pen and piece of paper and wrote the bill right there. The invoice read, "Turning screw: $1.00. Knowing which screw to turn: $999.00." You're going to discover which screw to turn.

"We will either find a way or make one."

HANNIBAL

We've all heard the saying, "Possession is nine-tenths of the law." Well, when it comes to eliminating Sore Spots, "Awareness is nine-tenths of the solution." Becoming aware of the Sore Spot is the first step. From my experience, acknowledging the Sore Spot is about ninety percent of the work. Why? Most people don't want to admit they're doing something that is harmful or destructive to the relationship, even if they're doing it subconsciously. Most people take the easy way out and blame their partner.

Ask not what your relationship can do for you, ask what you can do for your relationship.

We tend to believe if there is a problem, it's something our partner is doing, and if only he'd stop doing that everything would be better. So getting people to admit to and become aware of their contribution to the Sore Spot is most of the battle. You can't change another person. If you want your partner to change his behavior it is you that has to change your behavior first. If you change your behavior he will *have* to change his or leave the relationship because what he's doing will no longer work. To paraphrase President John F. Kennedy, ask not what your relationship can do for you, ask what you can do for your relationship.

Sore Spots represent where our childhood needs were not met. As adults, these Sore Spots make us ask questions like, "Why do I attract the same kind of guys?" "Why do I yell at my boyfriend or get so upset?" "Why do I wimp out and let him have his way all the time?" "Why do I need to be in control all the time? " "Why can't I say 'no'?"

WHAT A TRIP

When you walk, do you look directly beneath you where your feet are in that moment? No, you are always looking three or four steps ahead. You rarely look back from where you came, unless you tripped, and then you only look back to see what it was you tripped over so you won't trip on it again. If we applied this same concept to our relationships, we would be much happier with our relationship and our partner. We're going to look back at where you tripped so you won't trip any more.

> *"Do not look where you fell,*
> *but where you slipped."*
> AFRICAN PROVERB

When I was in school, I'd find other things to do when I didn't want to do my homework. I'd go workout, clean my room, clip my nails, or find anything else to do to postpone the inevitable. People do the same thing in their relationships. They buy a new sofa, buy a new car, or buy her a bigger ring to try and distract them or cover up the fact that the relationship is falling apart and they have these huge cracks in the foundation that they're not dealing with. On the outside everyone sees how "perfect" the relationship is. They say things like: "Look at how well they're doing. Look at the ring on her finger. Look at the new house. Look at the car they drive." To outsiders it's the portrait of a perfect relationship. But it's all a charade. They're trying anything to distract themselves rather than deal with the issues.

> *"Romance and work are great diversions*
> *to keep you from dealing with yourself."*
>
> CHER

Often when a relationship ends we blame it on our partner. That Sore Spot came up again in the relationship, and we know something is wrong, but we don't know exactly what it is or what we should do about it. We think it has to do with something outside of us, so we make changes. We change dating services, find someone younger, older, smarter, or dumber until we think we're ready to fall in love again. It'll be different this time for sure, we think. But, as the relationship evolves we find ourselves in familiar territory once again. Why? We made the same mistakes again. We changed everything but what *we're* doing. Only when you stop doing what you're doing, when you stop making those mistakes, can you find the relationship you're looking for. You stop making those mistakes by recognizing the Sore Spot and eliminating it.

CLEAN UP YOUR OWN BACKYARD

Temple University founder, Russell Conwell, told the story of a wealthy farmer who had heard stories of diamond fields that contained more diamonds than the world could ever use. Tantalized by the potential riches, the farmer sold his far and went in search of these mythical diamond fields. For years he searched high and low, far and wide, but never found the diamond fields. After years of searching, he died alone and penniless thousands of miles from home. The sad part is it wasn't long after the new owner moved in that he discovered acres of diamonds on the farmer's own land.

Your diamonds are not in some foreign land far, far away. They are right under your nose. If you want a better relationship you don't have to look any further than where you are.

*"We cannot connect with others
until we connect with ourselves."*

PEGGY COLLINS

Here's why you want to look inside yourself first: The abuse, neglect, abandonment, or criticism that we suffered in childhood has created a Sore Spot in our adult relationships. For example, if your parents ignored or punished you for speaking up, your Sore Spot may appear as the belief that no one really cares what you have to say. So you keep quiet and let others make all the decisions. Or, if you were rejected as a child, your Sore Spot may be automatically feeling personally rejected when a loved one rejects the sweater you gave him for his birthday. This is a subconscious behavior and it's a Sore Spot.

So, we'll look at how what you learned as a child may cause you to behave Destructively in relationships. You will find answers to questions like, "Why do I get so upset when he comes home late?" or "Why can't I stand up to him?" or "Why do the tiniest things make me react so violently?" or "Why do I pick all the wrong guys?"

We take what we saw, heard, and experienced from observing and interacting with our parents and generalize those observations to all our future relationships. So, it's not what you're partner's doing, it's *how you learned to respond to what he's doing* that is causing the Sore Spot. You will come to understand how the Sore Spot was created and why it keeps happening. What you'll discover will allow you to get rid of that Sore Spot and replace it with a Sweet Spot instead.

We take what we saw, heard, and experienced from observing and interacting with our parents and generalize those observations to all our future relationships.

In the chapters that follow you will be asked to answer questions and write out your answers in detail and with complete honesty. People get better by talking or writing out issues. This is why some people talk endlessly about their problems. It makes us feel better and allows us to regain control over something we felt we had no control over at the time. Talking it through allows us to regain control and overcome the issue.

Physician Larry Dossey would have his headache patients keep a diary of their headaches. By doing this he found that his patients' headaches disappeared. Children who experienced epileptic seizures were videotaped as they played in a room with one another. It was discovered that the kids would usually have seizures following emotional outbursts. When the children viewed this videotape their seizures dissipated. Why?

By keeping a diary or a journal, the person is able to view her condition in relationship to the grander scheme of her life. She is able to notice the overall pattern in her life and, as a result, change the pattern. By focusing on wholeness and oneness instead of separation and isolation, we become healthier and more complete. Writing in a journal brings that overall Sore Spot pattern into your awareness. It makes you conscious of the Sore Spot and allows you to change it. The people who learn from their patterns rarely repeat the same mistakes. Those who don't learn from their mistakes wind up spinning their tires and feeling more frustrated.

It's not what you're partner's doing, it's how you learned to respond to what he's doing that is causing the Sore Spot.

3

Normal Is As Normal Does

"There is no normal life, Wyatt. There's just life."

DOC HOLLIDAY
TOMBSTONE

YOU SEEM SO FAMILIAR

Let me destroy a myth right off the bat. We don't marry our parents. We marry someone who treats us like our parents did or lets us treat them the way our parents treated us. Most of our expectations and behaviors in relationships are formed at an early age. How our parents treated and responded to each other taught us how to give and receive love and attention. This became the "normal" way to get attention or what we're used to. If our parents were aloof and unemotional toward us, then we'll come to believe that acting this way is how to express love. As adults, we'll seek partners who are emotionally unavailable or we'll act that way toward our partners.

When parents criticize, ridicule, humiliate, or abuse they say, "I'm only doing this because I love you," or "This is for your own good." So we learn very early that we need to be criticized, humiliated, or abused in order to be worthy of our parents' love. As adults, we feel that being yelled at, humiliated, criticized, controlled, and punished by people who "love" us is normal. It's not normal. It's a Sore Spot.

If Mom told Dad she loved him and then turned around and belittled him, we got the message that it's okay to humiliate the one we love. When Mom caught Dad cheating but pretended it didn't happen, we learned that we shouldn't rock the boat and that our happiness and self-esteem don't matter. This directly affects our adult relationships because we either model or avoid doing what our parents did.

We marry someone who treats us like our parents did or lets us treat them the way our parents treated us.

MODELING 101

If you were able to distinguish between "right" and "wrong," you may have chosen to rebel and do the opposite of what that parent did. You may have chosen to stand up for yourself rather than allow any man to demean or humiliate you. You may have chosen to accept and love your partner unconditionally rather than using manipulation or abuse to control. No matter what the decision, it impacted every relationship you've had from the time you made that decision to now. If you saw Dad demean and humiliate Mom and had no other adult relationship to compare it to, then your decision was based on what you knew at the time.

"A man usually marries because he wants to "cure" his mother."

CARY GRANT

So it's not really shocking that you wind up dating or married to someone who treats you like your parents did or who lets you treat him like your parents treated you. If your parents disregarded your feelings when you were upset and you felt unloved, you came to believe that not showing your emotions is how to be worthy of love and attention. When your partner gets mad or feels guilty for not visiting his mother more frequently you devalue his emotions as your parents devalued yours. Or you find someone who disregards your feelings just as your parents did. You'll either find someone who treats you as your parents treated you or allows you to treat him as your parents treated you.

We tend to attract partners who behave the opposite of how we react. Not the opposite of our personalities. The opposite of how we *react* in certain situations. This is because we play both the role of parent and child within the relationship. For instance, during an argument we may allow him to demean and belittle us because that's how our parents treated us when we spoke our opinion. Later, when he wants a hug, we may deny him in much the same way our parents denied us. In both cases we are only doing what we learned to do from our childhood.

If you are emotionally void, your partner may be an emotional basket case. You disregard his feelings and call him too emotional and weak. Then, on the rare occasion that you become emotional, your partner may disregard your feelings because you ignore his and because he believes you've probably got everything under control, as you normally seem to do. Either way, he's disregarding your feelings just like your parents did years ago.

As adults we respond to certain situations according to what we learned as children. We learn how to respond to situations as adults by recalling three things from our childhood:

1. How our parents reacted to a similar situation.
2. How we reacted to a similar situation as a child.
3. How our parents reacted to us in that situation.

We rely on our parents and ourselves to determine how to respond in certain situations. If your parents reacted Destructively, then we more than likely will not react in a Constructive manner. Constructive responses may seem foreign to us. On the other hand, these Destructive reactions are familiar to us, so we repeat them until they become habitual behaviors or Sore Spots. Unless we become aware of the Sore Spot and commit to healing it, we will continue to make the same mistakes over and over again.

The good news is behavior is learned. The better news is if it can be learned, it can be unlearned. You weren't born frustrated. You had to learn how to respond in a frustrated manner. That behavior can be changed or unlearned.

"The definition of insanity is doing the same thing over and over and expecting different results."

BENJAMIN FRANKLIN

You don't need to read the numerous studies that have been conducted to know we do what our parents do. We see it growing up and we see it every day. Children become like their parents in an effort to feel more worthy of receiving love from Mom and Dad. At the subconscious level, the child is thinking, "If I become like my parents, they will love me more." We've seen abused children hit other kids on the playground when they don't get their way. We see a child yelling at another child because one child isn't playing the "right" way. As we grow up, we take these behaviors with us and use them in our adult relationships.

Sometimes we resent one or both of our parents and so we do the opposite of what they do out of spite. Even though what the parents are doing is appropriate and Constructive, we'll do the opposite because of this chip on our shoulder. So we end up behaving Destructively as a way to show our parents how independent we are. Obviously this is counterproductive, but when emotions are running high, all the logic in the world won't make a dent.

Subconsciously, we want to be treated like our parents treated us because it's what's most familiar. However, consciously we want a fairy-tale romance. It's the ultimate showdown between logical and emotional thinking. The logical mind thinks, "Take what you know, what's familiar. There's no such thing as happily ever after." While emotionally we're thinking, "But I want what she's got. I want the glass slipper."

"You cannot teach a person anything;
you can only help him find it within himself."

GALILEO

Also, be aware that true love doesn't heal Sore Spots nor can your partner fix your past. He simply has no clue how to heal your Sore Spot. Besides, he's got his own Sore Spot to worry about. You are the only one who can do anything about it. Until you do, that Sore Spot will come up again and again in your relationships. It's time to stop carrying that heavy emotional backpack. The sooner you eliminate the Sore Spot, the sooner you raise the quality of your relationship. You are the only one who can eliminate your Sore Spot. No one can do it for you, not even a therapist. The most anyone can do is guide you to where you need to be. Then it's up to you to heal your Sore Spot.

It's very popular nowadays to say you don't need to know *why* you do something, but to just stop doing it. Radio and television therapists across the land hurl their high and mighty attitudes at us saying, "get over it" or "do the right thing." And you know what, I agree with them. I know people can change in an instant. Unfortunately, those who do are usually the ones who experience something catastrophic, like hitting rock bottom or having a heart attack. The rest of us just keep plodding through our relationships, knowing things aren't great, but unsure of how to make it better.

I've come to realize that we need to find meaning in our obstacles. In order to change, we need to know *why* we behave a certain way and *how* to stop doing that. When you understand why you do something that's causing problems in the relationship, you are better equipped to stop the behavior. Once you've discovered the meaning, then it's time to "get over it."

I want to be clear that we're not blaming your parents. That's not what this is about. They were doing the best they could from what they learned from their parents. That will become very clear as we go on. Having said that, I'm going to use the term "parents" throughout this book. If you had guardians, stepparents, foster parents, grandparents, older siblings, or someone else raise you please make the adjustment.

Also, you need to know that a Sore Spot can develop in anyone from all types of backgrounds. Sometimes the person who had the worst possible childhood grows up to be respectful and loving, while the nurtured and loved child turns out to have a Sore Spot the size of Texas. Sore Spots are not dependent upon having a bad childhood, the worst parents, or a dysfunctional family. The truth is all families are dysfunctional to some degree. There are plenty of healthy, loving, and caring partners who grew up in dysfunctional families. What determines a Sore Spot is what you saw, heard, and experienced in your interactions with your parents, the decisions you made at the time, and how you and they responded to those interactions.

There are no normal relationships.
There are just relationships.

WALK A MILE IN MY SHOES

A father brought his young son to the local guru to help the boy overcome a problem. "Guru," the father said, "My son won't stop eating sweets. He refuses to eat anything but sweets and I'm afraid it will soon affect his health. I've tried being logical, I've grounded him for a week, I've ranted and raved like a lunatic, and I've begged him to stop eating sweets. I've tried everything, but I just can't get through to him. Can you do something?" The guru smiled and said,

"Come back in two weeks." Surprised but unquestioning, the father and son left. After two weeks the father and son returned. The guru smiled and said, "Very well. It is time to begin." But the father was curious and asked the guru, "I mean no disrespect, but why did we have to wait for two weeks?" Again, the guru smiled and said, "I needed two weeks because of *my* weakness for sweets. I knew I couldn't possibly help your son until I conquered my own issue."

I'm not asking you to do anything I haven't already done myself. I developed this program to get rid of my worst and most Destructive Sore Spots and I still use it whenever a minor Sore Spot appears. That's the idea. Get rid of the major Sore Spots so you can enjoy a better relationship. Then, use this program as a maintenance guide from time to time as needed. The more you review the messages contained in these pages, the more you glean from it because you'll hear or understand things you didn't get the first time.

"If you give people light they will find their own way."

DANTE

THE BUTTERFLY EFFECT

Research meteorologist Edward Lorenz developed a computer program that modeled the weather. One day Lorenz decided to reproduce a weather pattern from a previous test so he typed in the numbered coordinates from an earlier printout. When he did something strange occurred. The new printout produced a wildly different weather pattern than the one prior. He soon realized that the error was in the numbers he typed into the computer.

His printout only showed coordinates to the thousandth position, such as .643. But the computer's internal memory used numbers up to the millionth position, such as .643127. Lorenz quickly discovered such a minute change produced an enormously different outcome. This is what came to be known as the Butterfly Effect. It means that the infinitesimal changes created by a butterfly flapping its wings in Beijing have the power to create a hurricane in Florida. For you and me it means making very small changes to what we're doing in our relationships will have dramatic results. That's why it's so important to focus on these subtle adjustments so you can experience the incredible changes for yourself.

Making very small changes to what we're doing in our relationship will produce dramatic results.

Be aware, though, this program isn't going to make you change overnight. It's not like flipping a light switch on or off. No program in the world is able to do that. I tell you this ahead of time because you need to know the mind doesn't work that way. It took years of reinforcing the old habit, and it may take a bit of time to reinforce the new habit until it becomes a subconscious behavior. But it won't take years. If you do the work in this program, if you apply what you've learned, you will find new ways of relating to your partner immediately, and you'll be able to raise the quality of your relationship from day one.

When you complete this program, I recommend you continue using the guided imagery that you'll experience at the end of the program for twenty-one days. Studies have shown it takes twenty-one days to create a new habit and for the mind to assimilate it's new thought patterns. Just remember, little adjustments will create huge changes in your relationship.

> *"The first step to getting out of a hole*
> *is to stop digging."*
> PROVERB

This is not just a method or a process. It is a mindset, a mentality, or a way of thinking. It is a lifestyle. In order to create this new mindset you must go through these steps and understand how the Sore Spot was created and how you can heal it. More importantly, it's about following up for twenty-one days to create a new, Constructive habit.

That Sore Spot is simply a habit. Habits are just conditioned behaviors that we create so we don't have to consciously think about them each time we repeat them. It's like the smoker who gets the cigarette out of the pack, in his mouth, and lit without even thinking about it. The habit has become so ingrained that he's not even aware he's smoking.

Following the steps in this program will allow you to make a new decision that will have Constructive consequences. That new decision will affect every relationship you have from this point forward. You made the best decision you could as a child. Knowing what you know now you may never have made that decision. Yet that decision served a purpose at the time. It no longer serves that purpose and that is why it is creating problems for you in your relationships, problems that you can eliminate now.

As the story ends we see Cinderella completing this program and, realizing she can heal her Sore Spot, she makes subtle changes to what she thinks, feels, and how she behaves toward Prince Charming. In no time at all Cinderella and Prince Charming experience incredible changes to their relationship. Their relationship grows stronger as they realize how rewarding it is to communicate clearly by stating their wants, needs, and desires. The happy couple now relishes their differences of opinion and sees it as an opportunity to learn from each other and deepen their connection. By identifying, understanding, and eliminating their Sore Spots, Cinderella and Prince Charming discover what 'happily ever after' really means.

"To eat an egg, you must break the shell."
PROVERB

QUESTION 1

What is your Sore Spot? What is it that keeps popping up in relationship after relationship or in your long-term relationship again and again? What is the issue that, if you were to get to the root of it, the rest of your issues would disappear?

Examples:
I get frustrated.
I pout.
I throw tantrums.
I become passive.
I always have to be right.

_____

_____

_____

Feeling angry and acting out of anger are two different things. So we must distinguish between a feeling and the behavior that comes from that feeling. If your Sore Spot is a behavior, go to question #3. If your Sore Spot is an **emotion** like anger, sadness, fear (fear of commitment), guilt, frustration, jealousy, insecurity, loneliness, helplessness, hopelessness, hurt, feeling rejected, and so on, then answer this question:

QUESTION 2

What do you do or how do you respond when you're feeling _____? Feeling _____ causes you to react how, exactly?

Examples:
I lash out.
I Pout.
I keep it inside until I explode.
I try to be the life of the party or the center of attention.

_____

_____

_____

NOTE: Not expressing an emotion is still a behavior. If you are withholding or not expressing something, ask yourself, "Not expressing or holding it in for what purpose?"

Examples:
To keep the peace.
To avoid conflict.
So he doesn't leave me.

_____

_____

_____

Now that we know that your Sore Spot is a **behavior** like pouting, dominating, or being too needy and dependent, answer the following question.

QUESTION 3

When specifically do you respond this way? In what specific situations does your Sore Spot appear?

Examples:
When the house is a mess.
When he ignores me.
When I don't get my way.

_____

_____

_____

4

Addicted To Love

"Love doesn't make the world go 'round.
Love is what makes the ride worthwhile."
FRANKLIN P. JONES

EARTH ANGEL

Russian author, Leo Tolstoy, told the story of an angel who disobeyed God. As punishment, God stripped the angel of his wings and sent him, naked and alone, to a courtyard in the dead of winter. A shoemaker happened to be walking by, and not realizing the naked man was really an angel, invited the angel to stay with him. The shoemaker offered to provide room and board for the angel if he would help him make shoes. The angel eagerly agreed.

One day, after many years, the angel displayed such a smile that a heavenly light glowed about him. The surprised shoemaker asked the angel for an explanation. The angel told him his story and explained that the only way God would let him back into Heaven was if he discovered what made humans do the things they do.

He said he got his first lesson the day he was saved from the freezing cold. From his experience with the shoemaker, and through his interaction with others over the years, the angel came to realize that human beings aren't as selfish as he first thought. He noted that people need each other and that human beings cannot be happy unless they are able to love and be loved in return.

This story highlights our two greatest needs as human beings:

1. To be **loved**

2. To feel **worthy**

We'll focus more on feeling worthy in the next chapter. For now, just know that when we feel worthy we feel we are lovable. If we feel we're not worthy, we'll feel that no one will love us. Love is what we live for. Our yearning for love is what makes us look the other way when red flags begin to pop up early in the relationship. Love is what makes us miserable when we're apart or when it's missing. Love is the primary reason everyone on this planet is happy, sad, angry, jealous, anxious, hurt, reassured, guilty, frightened, frustrated, or walking on cloud nine. Each of us needs someone to love and someone who'll love us back. This is why we seek out and create relationships.

> *"We live by encouragement and die without it –*
> *slowly, sadly, angrily."*
>
> CELESTE HOLM

MONKEY LOVE

Have you ever felt lonely and cuddled with a teddy bear or a pet or even a pillow? Why does this make us feel better? At the University of Wisconsin in the 1950's, psychologist Harry Harlow conducted landmark experiments with baby monkeys. He found that when a baby monkey was deprived of his mother's touch the infant would become anxious and socially insecure. Harlow built two surrogate mothers: one out of warm, soft terry cloth and the other from cold, hard wire. Deprived of a real mother, the infant was forced to choose between the two and picked the cloth surrogate over the cold wire surrogate every time. When milk was only provided on the cold wire "mom," the infant would nurse on the wire surrogate but went right back to the warm, cloth "mom" for comfort when he was done feeding.

Harlow then took it a step further. He gave the infants only one choice: the cold wire surrogate "mom." Only this time it had sharp spikes sticking out of it. He also rigged the wire surrogate so that it would punish or abuse the infant by dousing him with cold water or hitting him with blasts of freezing cold air that would send the infant hurtling backward against the hard cage wall. Despite the abuse, the infants kept climbing back on 'mom' looking for more of the abuse that they misinterpreted as love and attention.

Each of us needs someone to love and someone who will love us back.

Researchers at Ohio State University studied the effects of a high cholesterol diet in rabbits. Groups of rabbits were fed high cholesterol foods. But the researchers noticed that one group of rabbits did not experience the hardening of the arteries that all the other rabbits experienced. After searching for answers, they discovered the lab technician responsible for feeding this group would take each rabbit out of its cage and pet it before he fed it the bad diet. In response to this love and attention the rabbits metabolized the diet differently and were able to avoid heart disease.

"I've learned that you cannot make someone love you. All you can do is be someone that can be loved. The rest is up to them."

AUTHOR UNKNOWN

It's a fact that premature babies who are caressed and stroked gain an average of 49% more weight than those who are not given such love and attention. People who live alone are less lonely if they have a pet. The pet offers an outlet for love and, as you know, pets give us love in return. It's pure, it's unconditional, and it's necessary for our wellbeing.

> *"There is only one happiness in life,*
> *to love and be loved."*
> GEORGE SANDS

Linguists estimate there are 6,809 different languages spoken on this planet. We may not understand each other's words, but we always understand each other's touch. Love, security, comfort, and care as well as hostility, anger, and indifference can all be communicated through touch. If deprived of love and attention a child may think, "If Mom and Dad wouldn't touch me I don't see how anyone else could." As an adult she may put up a "No Trespassing" sign to avoid deep intimacy with others or she may use sexual promiscuity to compensate for the lack of love and attention she experienced as a child.

> *"The greatest pleasure of life is love."*
> WILLIAM TEMPLE

H2-OH!

We know the average human body is made up of approximately 80% water and that it serves to transport energy throughout our body. A Japanese doctor by the name of Masaru Emoto conducted brilliant experiments and made some incredible discoveries about water. In his incredible book, *The Hidden Messages In Water*, Dr. Emoto explains how he photographed water molecules as they began to freeze. When water begins to freeze each molecule forms crystals. What he didn't realize is that our thoughts, or more specifically our intention, has a direct affect on water and the type of crystals that are formed. When Dr. Emoto wrote words on a label and put the label on a jar of water, the crystals from that jar would form according to the intention or word on the label.

For instance, the exclamation, "Let's do it!" created stunning crystals. If the command, "Do it!" was given, however, the molecules barely formed crystals at all. The words "love" and "gratitude," in *any* language, formed the most stunningly beautiful crystals. "I'm sorry," "You're cute" and, "Thank you" all formed beautiful crystals. Hateful words formed incomplete crystals and sometimes didn't form crystals at all. Loving, kind, and gracious words formed beautiful crystals every time and it didn't matter in what language they were written. This means it's not just the word; it's the intention behind the word that affects our bodies and our relationships. It's the thought that affects the water molecules that comprise your body. Is your intention kind and loving or is it mean and hateful?

In one particular study they filled three glass jars with water, put rice in each jar, and then every day said, "Thank you" to one jar, said "You fool" to the second jar, and ignored the third jar altogether. The rice that was told 'thank you' started to ferment into rice wine. The rice that was taunted with 'you fool' decayed and turned black. Most importantly, and more stunningly, the jar that was ignored actually rotted *before* the water that was told 'you fool.' What does this mean? It means we can handle being ridiculed a lot easier than we can if we're being ignored. This is why Harlow's monkeys as well as human children accept abuse and consider it love. It is better to receive *some* kind of attention, even if it's abusive, than none at all. For a child, it is most damaging when you withhold your attention.

"You really shouldn't say, "I love you"
unless you mean it. But if you mean it, you
should say it a lot because people forget."

JESSICA – Age 8

We all need to feel that we're worthy and that we're loved. If either need is missing, or perceived as missing, we'll be miserable. Each of us needs to get love and attention in very specific ways. You may truly love me, but if you don't give me attention the way I received attention as a child I will feel you don't really love me.

It is better to receive some kind of attention,
even if it's abusive, than none at all.

For instance, if as a child, I discover that by making a bigger deal out of things than they really are I get attention from Mom and Dad, I'll continue to make mountains out of molehills to get attention. Now, if you and I are dating and you don't buy into my melodrama, I won't feel loved by you. If I don't feel loved then one of my two greatest needs is not being met and one of my two greatest fears has come true. Just as we have two primary needs and almost everything we do is geared toward meeting those two needs, we also have two main fears. Just as our primary needs drive our behavior, these two fears dictate what we say and do as well.

"Loved people are loving people."

KATHARINE HEPBURN

5

The Sum of Our Fears

"The only thing we have to fear is fear itself."

FRANKLIN D. ROOSEVELT

Like our two needs there are also two fears that make us do the things we do. These two fears are:

1. I'm **not worthy**

2. I'm **not loved**

All fear is the fear of losing something and by losing something we feel we are less than we are. I can fear losing you, losing your attention, losing a companion, losing my freedom, and even losing my self-worth. If I lose something, like your attention, then I'll feel less worthy and unloved. If our two fears are predominant, we will do things to compensate for these fears and to make us feel more worthy and loved.

When we feel unworthy we feel we're not lovable. Who's going to love me if I'm not good enough? I have to be good enough in order for someone to love me. For instance, some people have to be right at any cost even if they know they're wrong. They fear that if they are wrong, then it will be found out that they are not worthy and therefore won't be loved.

At the same time, someone who lashes out isn't doing so because he's angry. He lashes out to cover up his fear of not being worthy. He's feeling less worthy because he has lost his sense of control. When we feel we have no control over our environment or ourselves, we feel less worthy. Subconsciously he knows that if he distracts you with his tantrum you won't be able to see through his façade. We control or give up control, argue or give in, whine or cry, or do whatever it takes to avoid our two fears and to satisfy our two needs.

These fears have control over us by making us feel safe from ridicule, humiliation, rejection, or embarrassment. These are all things that make us feel less worthy. If rejection makes you feel less worthy, you're going to avoid doing things that may lead to rejection. So, this fear might actually keep you from approaching and asking someone out on a date. The subconscious benefit for this fear is to keep you from being rejected. The problem is it keeps you from being accepted, too.

> *"The more of life you master,*
> *the less of life you fear."*
> PROVERB

If you want to avoid being hurt because getting hurt makes you feel less worthy, then the perceived subconscious benefit of keeping yourself safe will cause you to avoid getting too close to anyone emotionally. Did you get that? If I avoid getting close to you then I won't get hurt when you eventually leave me. The irony is while the *subconscious* benefit may help you feel more worthy in the short-term, in the long run you are *consciously* aware of the resulting frustration and loneliness but don't understand why you feel that way. These feelings then make you feel less worthy and less lovable. So, the very two things these fears are trying to prevent are exactly what they end up producing.

I believe everything can be broken down to self-worth or a lack thereof. Everything. When we feel we're not worthy we respond by feeling sad, irritated, angry, frustrated, jealous, and so on. We either lash out or retreat and feel sorry for ourselves. Remember, these feelings are only symptoms of what's really going on. When you find yourself feeling one of these emotions stop and ask yourself, "What is it that's causing me to feel like I'm not worthy? Is it a lack of control? Is it a lack of attention? Do I feel neglected, rejected, abandoned, or not needed?" Get to the bottom of why you're feeling that way. Take a moment before the emotion gets out of control and really ask yourself why you don't feel you're good enough at that moment. This is one of the best and easiest ways to not only learn more about yourself, but also to nip potential problems in the bud.

Every problem can be broken down to self-worth or a lack thereof.

So often we feel bad and immediately place the blame on someone or something else. We think if we're irritated it's because he's doing something that annoys us. It could be something as simple as someone bothering you in the mall. It's not that he's bothering you, but instead that he doesn't respect you enough to back off. Subconsciously you think, "If he doesn't respect me then I must not be worthy of respect. If I were more worthy he would listen to me and leave. Because he doesn't stop I must not be worthy." Of course consciously you're just thinking he's a jerk.

RHIANNON

Rhiannon was asked by her mother-in-law to plan a party, find a caterer, and invite all the necessary family and friends.

As she began planning, she discovered her mother-in-law was telling her who to call and how to do it. Every step Rhiannon took her mother-in-law was right beside her. She was trying to control every move Rhiannon made. Needless to say, Rhiannon was a bit irritated. "Why would she ask me to plan her party if she doesn't trust me?" she thought. "What does she need me for when she's doing it all herself?" She began to feel resentment toward her mother in-law so Rhiannon stopped and asked herself, "What's going on that's making me think I'm not worthy?"

After thinking for a moment she realized she felt irritated because she felt she wasn't needed. She recalled a memory from childhood when her own mother would brush her aside and take over whatever she was doing. Her mother would say, "If you want something done right you have to do it yourself." Because she didn't feel needed she began to feel she wasn't good enough, which caused her to feel resentment and anger. Lashing out, even if it's emotionally, is a defense mechanism learned early in childhood. The hidden message behind being angry with her mother-in-law was essentially, "I'll hurt you before you can hurt me." By feeling pushed aside Rhiannon took it as a personal affront so she pushed back, if only in her mind.

Once she got to the root of the problem she was able to come to grips with the whole experience because she knew in her heart that she didn't need her mother-in-law to need her. Rhiannon also realized her mother-in-law was controlling everything and everyone in order to feel more worthy herself. In the span of only a few minutes Rhiannon was able to diffuse her irritation and understand her mother-in-law a little better. If we take the time to uncover why it is we don't feel good enough in that moment, we can save ourselves a great deal of anxiety and worry.

"Come to the edge, he said.
They said: we are afraid.
Come to the edge, he said.
They came.
He pushed them...and they flew."
GUILLAUME APOLLINAIRE

A FEAR IS BORN

So how did these two fears come about? Where did they come from? They develop very early in our childhood from our interactions with our parents. If our parents had certain conditions or expectations that needed to be met before they expressed love, or they withdrew their love to punish us, it may make us feel we are not good enough or not worthy. We may come to believe that there's something wrong with us and we need to be fixed. We think, "If they won't accept me there must be something wrong with me."

When parents say things like, "Stop crying or I'll give you something to cry about," "Don't you get angry with me, young lady," "What are you so happy about?" or "Oh for God's sake, there's nothing to be afraid of" they squash any expression of emotion like anger, sadness, fear, excitement, or joy. We may then fear that expressing our emotions makes us unlovable, so we stop expressing our feelings and instead disconnect from any emotion and from ourselves.

If you were always told what to do rather than asked for your opinion, you may have become dependent or needy. Subconsciously you're thinking, "I'm not good enough to think for myself, so I'd better find someone who will make decisions for me. If I make a decision it'll probably be the wrong one, which means I'm not good enough, and therefore not lovable." The mother who tells you what to eat rather than letting you choose an item from the menu is subconsciously sending the message, "You're not good enough so I don't love you as much."

If your parents never allowed mistakes, or took over when you struggled and said, "Oh just let me do it" you may have learned to be a perfectionist and avoid making mistakes at any cost. The subconscious thought is, "If I make a mistake I won't be good enough, so I have to do everything perfectly. When I'm perfect I'll be worthy and then I'll be loved." Of course you may have done the opposite and simply don't try. What's the use in trying since you probably won't do it right anyway? The result is learned helplessness and a dependence on others to do things for you.

Are you beginning to see where, as a child, you made a subconscious decision to respond one way or another? That decision was made to make you feel more worthy and it has played a role in each of your relationships since then.

Depending on how your parents interacted with you, you may be constantly trying to prove your worth by being "perfect," being a helper, giving or taking control, or giving and giving and giving without expecting anything in return. We know once we're worthy we will be loved. Our two fears, then, cause us to behave in ways we feel we need to in order to feel worthy and loved.

Every issue in our relationships can be broken down to these two needs and these two fears. When we're loved it alleviates our fear of not being loved and not being worthy. When we don't feel loved our two biggest fears resurface and cause frustration, depression, anxiety, and feelings of hopelessness and helplessness.

It is through our thoughts, feelings, and behaviors that we continually strive to fulfill our needs and expect to feel worthy and loved. How we meet these needs is different for each of us because it all depends on how these needs were met as children. Every decision we make is based on our two needs and our two fears. We continually find ways to meet our needs but we're rarely conscious of how we do that. If we want to change our thoughts, feelings, or behaviors we must discover new, more Constructive ways of meeting our needs. However, if our behavior patterns are Destructive, we will fulfill our needs but feel frustrated, sad, angry, helpless, and so on. So, what's the difference between Constructive and Destructive behavior?

6

Good People Behaving Badly

*"What you do speaks so loud
that I cannot hear what you say."*

RALPH WALDO EMERSON

DESTRUCTIVE BEHAVIOR

Hurtful words and behaviors in the heat of the moment can damage a relationship, sometimes beyond repair. At the very least, it slowly eats away at the foundation of the relationship like those termites until one day it falls apart. Destructive behavior is harmful to the relationship. The easiest way to tell if what you're doing is Destructive is if you and your partner feel bad after acting a certain way. If you yell at your boyfriend because he didn't put the toilet seat down, chances are you're not going to feel very proud of yourself once you've cooled off.

Destructive behavior has no long-term benefits for you and is never beneficial for your partner or anyone else. Examples of Destructive behavior are being controlling, belittling, being verbally, sexually, emotionally, or physically abusive, bickering, arguing, pouting, giving the silent treatment, being too needy, using guilt to manipulate, and throwing tantrums.

You know it's Destructive behavior because it:

1. Never solves the problem.
2. Worsens the frustration you're feeling.
3. Makes you feel more worthy but only in the short-term.

The danger is if we feel more worthy, we'll continue to behave Destructively. People never do anything unless it meets a need and feeling more worthy certainly meets a need. Our minds do not distinguish between Destructive and Constructive behavior. The mind knows only that the need to feel worthy is being filled. It doesn't care how the need is met, just as long as it is. If you're starving, you're not going to hold out for your favorite meal. You're going to eat whatever is given to you. Once that need is satisfied the mind will continue to create that behavior because it knows the need will be filled. When the need stops being satisfied, the mind will look for some other way to meet that need.

"Most people prefer the certainty of misery to the misery of uncertainty."
VIRGINA SATIR

TINA

Tina feels neglected by Jim when he's on the computer, so she slams cupboards and stomps around the house, but Jim just continues working on the computer. Finally, she blows up and yells at him for not putting the clean dishes away. This obviously gets his attention. It is Destructive behavior because he is now on the defensive and they're in an argument that neither of them really knows what about.

On the surface, Tina feels better because she has his attention. But this feeling is superficial and temporary because arguing only increases her frustration and his resentment and it never addresses the real issue. Tina doesn't ask for him to pay more attention to her. Instead she drops hints by storming around the house and yelling at him. Jim begins to resent Tina because she isn't respecting his boundaries. He needs to get his work done, but she puts her needs ahead of his and interrupts what he's doing. Tina feels neglected and that makes her feel less worthy and ultimately unloved. Because the real issue is not addressed, this Sore Spot continues to eat away at the foundation of their relationship.

CONSTRUCTIVE BEHAVIOR

Constructively meeting your needs moves the relationship forward and has positive side effects for you and your partner. You know you are behaving Constructively if you feel good about it afterward. Let's take a look at a Constructive way of meeting a need.

BRETT & KATIE

Brett needs to feel excitement in the relationship so he surprises Katie with little notes and gifts every once in a while. Katie returns the favor by planning a trip to Hawaii for a second honeymoon. The bond grows stronger between the two of them because they both feel worthy and loved. They both give Constructively to the relationship and they grow closer as a result.

The brain doesn't distinguish between Destructive or Constructive behavior. It doesn't judge or decide which behavior is better or worse for us. So long as we feel worthy and loved, it doesn't care how. If our Destructive behavior is satisfying an emotional need we will do it again and again.

As human beings, we will never do anything unless we think it will make us feel more worthy and loved. That means that every behavior, whether positive or negative, appropriate or inappropriate, Constructive or Destructive, can be used as a means of satisfying our two needs. When in doubt ask yourself, "Does what I'm doing contribute to or take away from my relationship? Am I supporting or destroying the fabric of my relationship?"

When Tina argues with Jim in order to get attention, she is acting Destructively to satisfy her need to feel worthy and loved. Her behavior does not have a positive affect on her or Jim; they both feel bad. If Tina would communicate her needs clearly and calmly without verbally attacking Jim, he would be more receptive to her. Behaving Constructively is beneficial for both Tina and Jim and they both feel good about it afterward.

I'm not saying you should never speak up when you're angry, frustrated, or sad. It's very healthy to do so. But when it's Destructive and it happens in the same situations again and again it's a problem. It's a Sore Spot.

QUESTION 1

What Destructive side effects has this Sore Spot had for you
<u>and</u> your relationships?

Examples:
My relationships never last.
Everyone thinks I'm a bitch.
My boyfriend resents me.
No one takes me seriously.
He doesn't trust me anymore.

_____

_____

_____

_____

QUESTION 2

What is the ripple effect? What Destructive side effects has
this Sore Spot had on those around you, especially loved
ones (partner, spouse, siblings, children, parents, coworkers,
friends, neighbors, etc.)?

Examples:
They're tired of my constant drama.
My boyfriend never got to know the real me.
My family is disappointed in me.
My husband feels hurt.

_____

_____

_____

_____

QUESTION 3

What is the Silver Lining in all of this? If you could find at least one good thing that came out of all this, what would it be? How are you a better person today because of this Sore Spot?

Examples:
I spent time alone and discovered who I really am.
I developed my creative side.
I started my own business.

_____

_____

_____

_____

"Goliath was the best thing that ever happened to David."

DOUG WEED

BEHAVIOR vs. INTENTION

The intention to satisfy our two needs is always Constructive. Our behavior, on the other hand, may be either Constructive or Destructive. This is why we must separate behavior from intention. Obviously we have good intentions in our relationships; we just use Destructive behavior sometimes. The highest intention is always to feel more worthy and loved. The behaviors we use to satisfy that intention could be anything.

When Tina picks fights and argues with Jim, her behavior, arguing, is obviously Destructive; it's not good for her, Jim, or the relationship. Her intention, however, is Constructive in that she is looking to fill her need for attention. When she receives attention she feels more worthy and loved. When she fights with him she has his attention. Deep down inside she has a belief that arguing is the only way she can fill this need. It's what she learned growing up; it's what's "normal" and familiar to her. She could use a more Constructive approach by sitting down and discussing her issues with him, but in the heat of the moment she falls back on the familiar way of satisfying her need.

In his attempt to feel more worthy, Jason teases Carly to the point of being hurtful. When he teases Carly, subconsciously he feels superior and more worthy. He shrugs it off as just having a little fun but to Carly it's highly personal, degrading, and abusive. Carly responds Constructively to Jason's Destructive behavior by setting and enforcing her boundaries. She does so in a calm manner in which both feel respected and validated. By doing this, Jason doesn't get defensive and is open to hearing her concerns. Jason now has two options: respond Constructively or leave the relationship. He knows if he responds Destructively, Carly will most likely leave him. If she does leave, he'll feel less worthy and unloved. So he chooses to act Constructively. Carly feels more worthy and loved as a result and behaves more lovingly toward Jason. This makes him feel more worthy and loved and on and on it goes.

Remember, intention is always Constructive. Behavior can be either Constructive or Destructive. Be aware of everything you do. Are you doing it to feel loved? Are you doing it because you're afraid you're not good enough? It all boils down to avoiding our two fears and satisfying our two needs.

"To have the results you've never had, you must do what you've never done."

PIERRE DUCASSE

UP THE MOUNTAIN

We want to get to know the Sore Spot, that part of us that can behave Destructively, and we want to discover it's true intention. Remember, we must separate behavior from intention. There are no good or bad Sore Spots. All Sore Spots served a purpose at one time but no longer serve that purpose. Sore Spots are only harmful when they control us and they only control us when we're not aware of them. Even the most negative Sore Spot has a positive intention behind it. So let's discover the positive intention right now, together.

The following exercise can be done with any Sore Spot you wish to know more about. Whether it's the part of you that gets upset when someone forgets to take out the trash, or the part of you that feels guilty for bothering him while he's watching the game, you can use this imagery to learn more about that Sore Spot and understand its purpose and true intent. You should discover that no matter what the Sore Spot, its intention is pure.

NOTE: It's often more effective to listen as someone guides you through imagery. For this reason I have included "Up The Mountain," as well as the imagery at the end of chapter 13, on my CD called "Journey Back To You." It can be found at www.scottkudia.com.

Up The Mountain

Close your eyes and imagine walking with your Sore Spot toward a mountain path. What do you call your Sore Spot? It can have any kind of name at all. What does it look like? It may take the form of an animal, person, or an inanimate object like a rock or a glowing ball of light. What shape is it? What size is it? What color is it? Let it take whatever form it chooses. Just let it come to you without forcing it. Don't judge it. Let it appear and reveal itself to you. If it wants to change forms, let it. As you walk up the mountain, notice what feeling comes from that Sore Spot. It's okay if there is more than one emotion associated with the Sore Spot. Continue walking together up the mountain and let the Sore Spot speak to you. Let it express its needs, desires, concerns, and frustrations. Whatever it wishes to discuss, allow it without judging. Even if it's an inanimate object, it can speak and express itself to you.

As you continue to climb higher, notice the Sore Spot. Does it change size, shape, color, or into something completely different altogether? Allow it to take whatever form it chooses as you reach the peak of the mountain.

Stand together at the top and look out over the world below. As you do, you begin to feel a warm, peaceful, white light surround you and begin to fill every pore, every cell, and every molecule in your body. Notice the light surround and permeate the Sore Spot, as well. As you become one with the light, notice yourself becoming one with the Sore Spot, too. As the two of you become one with the purifying, soothing white light, allow the Sore Spot to reveal its true intention to you. Take a moment to integrate what you have experienced. When you're ready, come back to now and open your eyes.

QUESTION 4

What did you learn from your journey up the mountain? What's the positive intention behind your Sore Spot? What does that behavior do for you or give you? Does it make you feel worthy? Loved? Give you attention or a sense of control? What is the positive feeling you get by expressing the negative behavior? For instance, if you feel you have no control, then you may lash out to regain control. What's the positive intention behind your reaction?

Examples:
I feel important.
I get attention.
I feel like I matter.

_____

_____

_____

_____

_____

_____

_____

_____

_____

"What counts is not necessarily the size of the dog in the fight - it's the size of the fight in the dog."
DWIGHT D. EISENHOWER

I had an experience of walking up the mountain with a Sore Spot I called, "Ahhhh!" This Sore Spot consisted of doing things I didn't want to do in order to avoid any conflict. I never told anyone no. It looked like Mr. Hyde in a top hat and large coat. This Sore Spot told me it's intent was to make me feel more worthy. By avoiding conflict and agreeing to anything, the Sore Spot thought it was putting me in a position where others would like me. The intention was pure. The behavior, never saying 'no,' was Destructive because it left me feeling taken for granted and frustrated.

As we climbed, the Sore Spot became smaller and took the form of me as a child now wearing a huge coat and hat. It soon lost the coat and hat as we continued to the top. Once there, the light shone brightly and we held hands and communicated with each other. Then my younger me picked me up and we flew into the light together. It may sound simple enough, but the experience was very intense and enlightening.

A word of caution: If the Sore Spot you are exploring is something you cannot accept, it will not reveal itself to you. You must come to terms with it and accept that it is a part of you, it does serve a purpose, and it has a positive intention. Never judge it. Only then can it emerge and show its true form; only then can you change it. This guided imagery frees you from the control that Sore Spot had over you. It also serves to gain a better understanding of it. When we understand and learn from our Sore Spot, we regain control over it.

When it's just a habit we think, "I don't know why. It just sets me off." Just becoming aware of the Sore Spot changes it. It cannot be the same Sore Spot any longer because of our awareness. Now, when I don't want to do something, I remember, "It's okay to say 'no,' you'll still be liked." The very act of becoming aware of the Sore Spot means it has changed. Think about how differently you behave when you know someone is watching you. No matter how negative the Sore Spot seems there is always a positive intention. If you cannot determine it's positive intent, it is most likely because you are still at odds with it. If that's true, continue through the book, then come back to the exercise afterward.

When you listen to a symphony, see a play, or look at a painting, you don't think about how each of its elements helps to create one harmonious whole. In a symphony, all parts play together to create beautiful music. But if one part is off beat or out of tune, the whole symphony is ruined. We certainly notice when something is a little off or out of tune. Your relationship is your symphony. The Sore Spot is the instrument that's out of tune. Let's get it back in tune so you can create beautiful music again.

> *"It is not the mountain that we conquer,*
> *but ourselves."*
>
> SIR EDMUND HILLARY

Next, we're going to discuss our thoughts and how almost all of our thoughts are designed to avoid our two fears and fill our two needs. We'll see how our thoughts make us feel certain emotions and do certain things. Above all, we'll discover how our thoughts create the level of quality in our relationships and why we keep doing the same things again and again despite being harmful to the relationship.

7

The Mental Merry-Go-Round

"We are what we think.
All that we are arises
With our thoughts.
With our thoughts,
We make our world. "

THE BUDDHA

As we've discussed, we all have a fear of not being worthy and not being loved. But what is it that feeds these fears? What is it that causes one person to thrive and another to give in to their fears in relationships? The answer lies in the mind.

Do you know anyone who has sabotaged her relationships? Who has had the perfect relationship and lost it? Or has had sweet relationships go sour on them? On the outside it looks like rotten luck, a lousy partner, bad timing, or whatever. But what's really going on here?

THE ANSWER IS BLOWIN' IN THE WIND

Let me ask you a question. How do you know there's wind? You can't see the wind because it's invisible. So how do you know there's wind? You know it's there because you see the effects of the wind on your world. You see trees swaying, little old ladies chasing their hats, and clouds moving across the sky. You feel sand blown in your eyes and you hear it howling through the trees or whipping the shudders on the house. You can't see the wind but you sure see the results of the wind, don't you?

The same is true of our thoughts. Thoughts can take the form of beliefs, ideas, values, attitudes, opinions, decisions, goals, dreams, doubts, or fantasies. We can't see our thoughts, but we can see the effects or results of our thoughts on our relationship. So it is the invisible that creates the visible.

"He who goes out of his house in search of happiness runs after a shadow."

CHINESE PROVERB

THOUGHTS

Consider the story of The Great Mysterio, an escape artist who was famous for picking locks and escaping from any room, safe, trunk, handcuff, or jail cell. In fact, he had a standing challenge to anyone who could produce a lock he couldn't pick. One day, a top padlock manufacturer, Lock, Stock, & Barrel, took him up on his challenge. They said they had developed a lock that was impossible to pick and if attached to a barrier would be virtually impenetrable.

Never being one to back down from a challenge, The Great Mysterio accepted. However, he had one condition: No one could watch him pick the lock. Everyone agreed. They put the lock on a prison cell door, stripped The Great Mysterio down to his boxer shorts, searched him, and put him inside the cell. All of the reporters, photographers, and padlock executives stepped outside to wait. The masterful magician was given one hour to free himself.

After only fifteen minutes the reporters became anxious and peeked inside. To their surprise, there was the famed Mysterio still trapped inside the cell. Only now he had broken a sweat and was frantically trying to get out.

If you think about it most people go through their relationships locked in their cells of mediocrity. For many of them they can see the key to the lock. In some cases they can almost touch it. But they just can't quite have the relationship they want. The perfect relationship always seems just an arm's length away. So how do you unlock the door?

"The ancestor to every action is a thought."
RALPH WALDO EMERSON

THE MENTAL MERRY-GO-ROUND

I'd like you to take a moment and realize that every thought you've ever had, every decision you've ever made, every belief you've ever held have led you to where you are right now. Every thought, decision, and belief you've ever had has produced results in your relationships. Whether those results are the ones we want or not don't matter – they're still results. Marriage may be a result we wanted while getting dumped may be a result we didn't want. Whether it is wanted or not, marriage and getting dumped are both results that can occur in relationships. But what is it that influences the results we get in our relationships? The answer is our behavior. If you behave respectfully you'll get respectful results. If you behave angrily you'll get defensive or angry results.

And what is it that influences our behavior? If you said our feelings, you are correct. The emotions we feel affect our behavior. When you're sad you're going to act sad. You'll slump your shoulders, hang your head, frown, and stay in bed all day. But what is it that influences our feelings? The answer to that question is our thoughts. Our thoughts include all of our beliefs, attitudes, opinions, values, ideas, decisions, doubts, fantasies, and goals. Therefore, it is our thoughts that are ultimately responsible for the quality of our relationships. I call this The Mental Merry-Go-Round.

"Be master of mind rather than mastered by mind."

ZEN PROVERB

The Mental Merry-Go-Round is how all habits, good or bad, are created and reinforced. It's crucial to understand this process and how you can use it to eliminate your Sore Spot.

According to The Mental Merry-Go-Round, the three things you need to change in order to raise your relationship to a higher level are:

1. What you **think**

2. What you **feel**

3. What you **do**

What we think is influenced by our need to feel worthy and be loved and our fear that we aren't good enough and that we won't be loved. Because everything we do is motivated by these two needs and fears, they fuel each thought we have. The origin of every thought, then, can be traced directly to how much we believe we're worthy and loved.

"Life reflects your own thoughts back to you."

NAPOLEON HILL

The process looks like this:

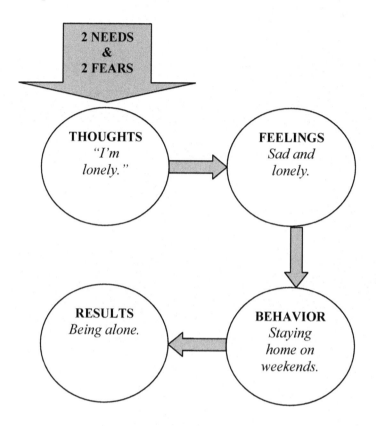

Our two needs and two fears make us *think* certain thoughts. Our thoughts cause us to *feel* a certain way. Those feelings make us *behave* a particular way. Our behavior then determines the *results* we get. *The results we get, whether we like them or not, will always reinforce our thoughts.* Read that last sentence again. So, if I think I'm lonely I may feel sad. Feeling sad makes me stay home on Saturday night. When I stay home I can't meet potential partners. The result is being alone. This result then reinforces my original belief that I'm lonely and creates a vicious cycle. The message is clearly, "what goes around comes around." The complete process looks like this:

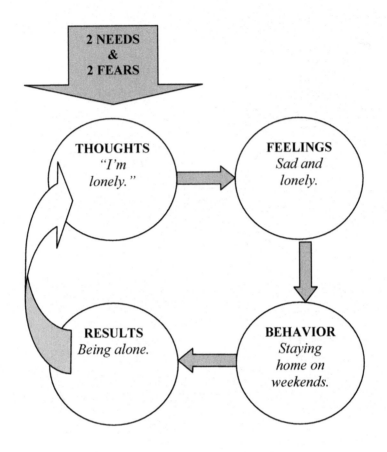

A thought in your mind creates a feeling that leads to behaving a certain way giving you a particular result. It comes full circle when the result you get automatically reinforces the original thought. If your thoughts are from a place of love then love will come back to you. If your thoughts come from a place of hate then hate will come back to you. In this way, we become our own worst enemy. Happiness brings more happiness. Sorrow brings more sorrow. Indifference brings more indifference. The message here is, "As you think so you become." You are what you think.

The results we get, whether we like them or not, will always reinforce our thoughts.

This is why I call it the Mental Merry-Go-Round. Some people love Merry-Go-Rounds and they enjoy riding them. These are the people who think predominantly Constructive, solution oriented thoughts. Other people become dizzy and get sick and want desperately to get off of the Merry-Go-Round. These people are predominantly Destructive, problem oriented thinkers.

If you plant a smelly onion you're not going to get a beautiful rose. You'll get a smelly onion. If you have hateful thoughts you're not going to get love in your life. You're going to get hate. That's The Mental Merry-Go-Round. You can never get off the Merry-Go-Round but you can learn to enjoy the ride. So how do you do that? You've got to start making some changes.

Do we start with the results? No. But most people try. When they don't get the results they want they focus more attention on their results. They say things over and over like, "I can't believe this happened" or "Why me?" or "This sucks. This really sucks." Focusing on an unwanted result isn't going to change it and will only make you feel worse about it. Having a rotten relationship is never, ever a problem. Why? Because having a rotten relationship is a *result*. If a problem exists it's in your thoughts and how those thoughts produce feelings and behaviors to create your results. Don't focus on the rotten relationship; focus on your thoughts.

"Take away the cause and the effect ceases."
MIGUEL DE CERVANTES

When you change your thoughts you change the emotions you're feeling which changes the way you behave. By

71

becoming aware of your thoughts you can begin the process of changing them. When you change your thoughts you literally change your relationship. Think about what happens when somebody's watching you. When someone is watching you, you become self-conscious and you behave differently. So do your thoughts. When you start watching your thoughts they begin to act differently; they begin to change. Your thoughts are the key to unlocking the door that leads to better relationships. Once you know which key to use the rest is easy.

If The Great Mysterio had known what you now know perhaps things would have been different. For, you see, after two hours the press came back inside only to find him physically and emotionally exhausted. The padlock company had won. And, as The Great Mysterio collapsed with fatigue against the cell door, it opened. The door was never locked. In case you didn't know, you can't pick a lock that isn't locked. In the chapters that follow, I'm going to show you how to determine which locks are real and which locks are all in your mind.

8

The Brain:
Your Personal
Search Engine

*"You are today where your thoughts
have brought you. You will be tomorrow
where your thoughts take you."*

JAMES ALLEN

Here's another reason you might want to become aware of what thoughts are running through your mind. In the 1920's, Canadian neurosurgeon Wilder Penfield operated on the brains of epileptics, stimulating specific areas of their brains with an electrode. When he stimulated certain areas of their brain, his patients relived specific events from their past in stunning detail. A man literally heard his mother talking on the phone from when he was a boy and was able to recite her conversation word for word. A woman remembered being in her kitchen and could actually hear her son playing outside despite the fact that she was in a hospital. From these amazing experiments, Penfield determined that everything that happens to us is stored in our brains as memory.

Then in 1946, neuropsychologist Karl Lashley trained rats to run a maze successfully. In an attempt to discover precisely where memory was stored in the brain, Lashley surgically removed portions of the rats' brains and put them through the maze again. However, he quickly found that no matter what part of the brain he removed, the rat was still able to run the maze. In fact, Lashley removed the entire brain except for the brain stem and despite suffering from uncoordinated motor function the rats were still able to complete the maze. Behold the power of cheese!

After reviewing these experiments, neurophysiologist Karl Pribram wondered how the rats were still able to run the maze despite having most of their brains removed. Pribram theorized that memory must not be stored solely in the brain but in the entire body as well. How is this possible?

YOU HAVE SOME NERVE!

Our body contains a network of nerve cells that act like information superhighways delivering messages to every nook and cranny of the body faster than email. If your brain notices you haven't eaten for a while it will send the message, "I'm hungry" to your stomach. The message is sent by an electric impulse from one nerve cell to another. Nerve cells are capable of wiring and rewiring themselves in order to transmit messages the quickest way possible.

The message gets passed along from cell to cell until it reaches its destination, the stomach. When the stomach receives the message it immediately responds by rumbling. It's sort of like taking the subway and changing trains two or three times, only the message changes nerve cells millions of times in a split second in order to reach its destination. In fact, a nerve cell can transmit between 500 and 1000 impulses each second.

The human body contains 30,000 million nerve cells, while the human brain has over one hundred billion nerve cells. If you were to place every nerve cell from your body end to end, it might create a chain over two hundred miles long. Even if you were dipped in a solution that stripped your body of everything but these nerve cells, when they pulled you out of the vat you're great aunt Sophie would still recognize you. Nerve cells are not just information superhighways. They are you.

This is significant because it reveals the mind-body connection. It means that at any given moment every thought you have is being directly communicated to every cell in your body in just a fraction of a second. When you're happy, your cells are happy. When you're sad, your cells are sad. Do you know anyone who has a bad back or a bum knee? How do you think your back feels when you say, "Bad back! Bad back!" How do you think your knee feels when you call it a bum?

"Our deepest fear is not that we are inadequate. Our deepest fear is that we are powerful beyond measure."

NELSON MANDELA

In his remarkable book, *The Hearts Code,* Dr. Paul Pearsall tells the story of a murdered ten-year old girl whose heart was transplanted into an eight-year old girl. Once recovered, the girl had a memory from the murdered girl's heart. From that memory the girl was able to give a description to police of the weapon, the clothes the killer wore, the time and place, and even what the little girl said to him just before he killed her. This evidence led to the capture and conviction of the killer. The cells from the murdered girls heart continued to transmit their message despite being in another girls' body.

Every thought you have gets directly communicated to every cell in your body.

Dr. Candace Pert, in her groundbreaking book, *Molecules Of Emotion*, says the body is inseparable from the mind. She says our bodies are not only made out of molecules but out of our experiences, as well. This means that the body *is* the mind. According to Pert the human body is designed to produce behavior based on what we focus on. That means your body today is the result of what you have focused on your entire life up until now.

The mind-body connection is thought. Who is in charge of your thoughts? You are in charge of your thoughts. If every cell is affected by everything you think, then what you believe is acted upon as if it were real. What you believe to be real is real. The mere act of thinking and believing a specific thought will cause the body to respond with a certain behavior. Remember the Mental Merry-Go-Round: Thought comes first, feelings and behavior follow.

Jill *thinks* she's ugly so she *feels* ugly and less worthy. This leads to *behaviors* like staying home and avoiding parties and other chances to meet men. When she does this it *results* in her being alone which reinforces her thoughts of being ugly. "Of course I'm alone," she thinks, "I'm ugly. Who'd date me?"

MAKE A CIRCUIT WITH ME

Do you remember those old movies where an operator handled a switchboard and, depending on where she plugged the cord, you could be talking to someone next door or to someone in Australia? Our neurology acts much like that switchboard operator. Nerve cells connect with other nerve cells in order to most efficiently send their messages throughout the body. The nerve cells literally rewire themselves in order to pass the message more quickly.

If you do something over and over, like thinking, "I'm stupid," yelling at your partner, or smiling whenever you think of him the connection between particular nerve cells will be strengthened. A strong connection means it has become a habit and you are less conscious of your response. If you think the thought one time, you may have only a few nerve cells rewiring themselves. If you never think that thought again, the nerve cells will break their connection. However, if you continue to think that thought again and again, you could potentially have millions of nerve cells forming one bond. The more nerve cells that form a particular connection, the stronger that bond will be. And each time that connection is reinforced it makes it easier for you to respond that way the next time. This is how habits are formed.

This also explains how the rats were able to successfully run the maze despite having most of their brain removed. The memory of successfully completing the maze was stored somewhere amongst the billions of nerve cells in their body. By running the maze over and over again they built a very strong nerve cell connection. So, when they had to run the maze again, they could do it without thinking. They had to. They no longer had a brain. Even though your brain is still in tact, you still do things without thinking, like brushing your teeth, driving to work, and walking.

When you first learned to walk your brain had to think about trying to keep you balanced, how and when to move each foot, using your arms for support or to break your fall, and looking toward where you were trying to walk - all at the same time. But eventually, as you began to walk more and more, the nerve cells sent messages back and forth until a strong connection was created in your brain. Now you can walk without thinking about it because the nerve cells have created and reinforced that "walking" connection.

Those rewired nerve cells are like an Internet search engine. They will give you exactly what you're searching for. Rewiring those nerve connections is kind of like typing in a different topic to search for on the Internet. Each time you type in that thought, you reinforce it. Reinforcing it is like giving that site more hits or visits. The site that has the most hits will be the first site listed when you conduct your search. The more often you visit or hit that site, the faster it ends up at the top of the search list. So you're brain, and all those nerve connections, basically act as your own personal search engine. A bundle of "angry" nerve cells will produce "angry" thoughts in similar situations in the future. That "angry" website in your brain has been hit so many times it's the first site listed when you see his dirty underwear on the floor.

Let's look at a simplified example. Grant and Sharon have been dating for a few months. During a seemingly harmless discussion of former lovers, Sharon mentions how she picked a guy up at a bar one night to get back at her boyfriend after a particularly heated argument. She goes on to tell Grant that she never told her ex because they made up the next day. Upon hearing this, the nerve cells that were once wired for trust begin to rewire with other nerve cells to form suspicious and non-trusting connections. The more Grant thinks about what Sharon might do should they ever argue, the stronger the union becomes between those nerve cells. Soon, the connections are so strong that he can no longer think trusting thoughts. Instead, he becomes paranoid and anxious every time she goes out with her friends. His internal search engine continuously brings back thoughts of infidelity, jealousy, suspicion, and anxiety.

If you get annoyed at your partner on a daily basis, you're inviting more and more nerve cells to join the rewiring party in your brain. Millions of nerve cells get rewired until that behavior is so unconscious that it becomes part of your definition of who you are. You can no longer see his underwear on the floor for what it is: dirty underwear on the floor. Instead, you see it as a slap in the face to you and your repeated requests that he put his dirty laundry in the hamper. Those rewired nerve cells have made it easier for you to become annoyed at any little thing he does that you don't agree with. Your internal search engine finds similar things that will annoy you like leaving the toilet seat up, leaving dirty dishes in the sink, and going out with his friends. As a result, you begin to see yourself as fed up, frustrated, angry, or resentful of him. "I can't stand it when he does that," becomes your mantra and part of your definition of who you are in that relationship.

If you are able to stop or interrupt that particular thought or behavior pattern, the relationship between nerve cells will be severed. Once that pattern is interrupted and you've stopped rewiring and reconnecting, then that behavior, being annoyed, will no longer be an automatic response. Those nerve cells will begin to rewire and reconnect with other nerve cells to support that new thought pattern. They will now create a different automatic response, like calmly putting the dirty underwear back in the drawer with his clean pairs. When you rewire, you change from the inside out. You'll discover how to interrupt that nerve cell connection in chapter fifteen.

When you rewire, you change
from the inside out.

Not only does this apply to what we think about our partner, more importantly, it applies to what we think about ourselves. Thinking, "I'm worthless" over and over will eventually define you because you'll eventually believe it. Why? Because your internal search engine will search for and provide you with things that remind you of how worthless you are. You'll think of things like getting dumped or rejected or sitting alone on a Saturday night. You'll stop seeing the things that reinforce your worthiness because you're totally focused on your unworthiness.

Having the same thought over and over strengthens the connection between those millions of nerve cells. If you stop having that thought, you will destroy the connection and your brain will begin rewiring to support your new thought pattern. This is why Candace Pert claims that the cell is the smallest unit of consciousness in the body. The thought directly influences the cell. The cell, then, influences what the body feels and, ultimately, how you respond or behave.

That nerve cell is what carries the new thought to its destination, whether it's the stomach, big toe, or just another location in the brain. If we never think that thought again, that nerve cell will begin to rewire itself with different nerve cells. But each time we rethink that thought more nerve cells join in the fun and make the connection stronger. It's kind of like a muscle. When you exercise a muscle it gets stronger and easier to lift the weight. If you stop exercising that muscle it weakens and gets smaller. The more you think that thought and the stronger that nerve connection becomes, the easier it is to think that thought and the harder it is to not think it. The less you think that thought the faster it begins to rewire itself.

By becoming aware of a Destructive thought, you can stop thinking that thought and get the nerve cells to rewire by thinking a more Constructive thought. Your thoughts lead to specific feelings and behaviors that create specific results. Those results always reinforce your thoughts, which further strengthens the connection making it harder to stop thinking that thought. It stands to reason, then, that you'll get more of the results you want if you begin with a Constructive rather than a Destructive thought. You'll discover how to identify and change Destructive thoughts in chapter 10.

"The pessimist sees difficulty in every opportunity. The optimist sees the opportunity in every difficulty."

SIR WINSTON CHURCHILL

SAME THOUGHT...DIFFERENT DAY

We think between sixty and ninety thousand thoughts each day. Roughly eighty percent of those thoughts are negative or Destructive. More importantly, we will re-think about ninety percent of today's thoughts tomorrow. In other words those nerve cells get a lot of exercise. So we can see rather easily how quickly we can get stuck in a negative pattern of thinking. Have you ever been singing lyrics to your favorite song and then found out the lyrics are different from what you've been singing? When you try to sing the song you may still sing the old lyrics but now you catch yourself. When you catch yourself enough times you eventually sing the correct lyrics without thinking about it. So it doesn't matter how strong the nerve connections are, they can be rewired if they lead to unwanted behavior and results.

Now, do you believe <u>what</u> you think will determine <u>how</u> you behave? Absolutely! If a little girl is told she's stupid by her parents and she begins to tell herself the same thing, she is creating an incredibly strong nerve cell connection. So strong, in fact, that she responds, "I'm so stupid" without even thinking about it. It has become a habit. What happens when you say or think something enough times? You start to believe it. The person who thinks she's stupid will act stupid and put herself in situations that make her look and feel stupid because her internal search engine is wired to give her what she's focused on.

What you believe to be real is real.

Growing up, Laurelei was continually told she was stupid by her parents. As an adult, despite being a brilliant businesswoman, her husband also calls her stupid. That's a lot of nerve cells forming that "stupid" connection. Now, when little things happen, like opening the refrigerator and having the ketchup bottle fall harmlessly to the floor, without hesitation she says to herself, "I'm so stupid." What you think about yourself will determine how you treat yourself and how others treat you.

> *"If we were to talk to strangers the way we talk to ourselves they'd punch us in the nose."*
> WILL ROGERS

Likewise, what you think about your partner will determine how you treat him. If you think he's too good for you, you may be constantly trying to prove your worth. Or, thinking he's incapable of accomplishing anything on his own, you may start to do things for him. Perhaps you think he embarrasses you, so you avoid bringing him to work functions or parties and you demean or belittle him when you're with him. If you don't think he's worthy of respect how can you treat him with respect? It all begins with a thought.

What you think about your partner, even if it's not true, will determine how you treat him.

Most people are not aware of their thoughts or do not believe that they control them. But if you don't control your thoughts, who does? If you don't control your thoughts then how can you change them? If you don't control your thoughts then you're powerless to control your own life. There is no magic genie putting thoughts in your head. There is only you.

9

Be Careful What You Wish For

"Drag your thoughts away from your troubles... by the ears, by the heels, or any other way you can manage it."

MARK TWAIN

WHEN "NO" MEANS "YES"

Don't think of Santa Claus. Whatever you do, do not think of Santa Claus. Now, what are you thinking of? You can't *not* think about what you don't want without first thinking about what you don't want. Think about it. An important aspect regarding the mind is that it does not process negatives directly.

Let's say I asked you, "Why do you want to get married?" and you said, "Because I don't want to date jerks anymore." In order for you to not want to date jerks, your mind has to make a picture of a jerk so it knows what you don't want. The mind has to make a picture of what it does not want in order to not want it. However, our neurology is designed to produce what we focus on. Therefore, the very act of creating a picture in our mind means we are focusing on it.

In the end, what will you get? That's right, the boyfriends who turn out to be jerks.

Remember the Butterfly Effect and how small changes create huge results? If you were to make a subtle adjustment to your thinking, you would experience a profound change in the results you get. Now, let's say I asked why you want to get married and you said, "Because I want to be with my soul mate." Your mind now creates an image of your soul mate and you are focusing on what you *want* rather than what you *don't want*. Your mind moves toward what you want by creating the picture of your soul mate.

The mind does not process negatives directly. How many times have you said, "Don't look now" and what's the first thing he does? Parents understand this when they tell their children, "Don't play in the street." Of course the kids are thinking, "The street? I never thought of that. Let's go!" Will your boyfriend call if you say to him, "Don't forget to call me?" It's better to say, "Remember to call me later."

This is why, when the struggling couple decides to reconnect by going away together for a long weekend, they end up not speaking the entire time. In theory that's all very nice. In reality, if they are still focused on the negative aspects of each other and do nothing to resolve them, they will be no better off than if they had stayed home. Going away with each other will only make matters worse if they're still focused on what they don't want. That internal search engine keeps spitting out thoughts that reinforce their frustration. Will she feel like reconnecting with him when she notices he left the toilet seat up again, burped in the restaurant, and hums while he chews his food? If she's focused on the things that annoy her, she won't feel very loving toward him and she won't enjoy her ride on the Mental Merry-Go-Round.

Because the mind does not process negatives directly and our nervous system is designed to give us what we focus on, it is important to focus on what you want. Even though you may long for someone who doesn't burp, since you're focused on the burper, you're more likely to end up with him.

Furthermore, if you're not focused on what you want you'll either deny what you want is actually there or you'll think, "It's too good to be true" or "It won't last." Worse still, you may happily accept it when it appears only to have your Sore Spot eventually sabotage it.

"Where there is negative thought
let there be reflection to the contrary."
PATANJALI

CRAB IN A BUCKET

I tell my clients to hang out with people they want to be like rather than those they do not. This is because the people we hang out with help to create what we focus on. If you want to settle down with a husband in a quiet country home but are living in the city hanging around friends who date everyone they meet and party every night, you could be in for disappointment. Your dream will remain a dream because the people you hang out with aren't going to challenge you to achieve your dreams. They'll be focused on drinking and clubbing and partying and so will you. This is called Crab In A Bucket Syndrome.

Did you know fishermen don't have to place a lid on a bucket full of crabs? This is because when one crab begins to crawl out the other crabs pull him back in. Misery truly does love company. If it didn't, there would only be one fly on a fly strip waving to the others and shouting, "Go around!"

Now, this does not mean that you should go out and get a whole new group of friends. However, you should be conscious of who you're hanging out with. The people you hang around will create what you focus on. If you don't want to be like them, don't hang around them as much. It's okay to party once in a while. But you're probably not going to meet a guy who values settling into the quiet life at a rave party or mosh pit. Be aware of the people you're hanging around and how they affect you.

> *"Do not listen to those who weep and complain, for their disease is contagious."*
>
> OG MANDINO

PROBLEM vs. SOLUTION THINKING

If you're walking barefoot down a path and you step on a thorn, you could hop around and focus on the thorn and how much it hurts. But that only makes it worse. You could, instead, focus on possible solutions. When you do, you may get the idea to use another thorn to remove the one in your foot. It's your choice whether you focus on the problem or the solution.

Problem thinking is Destructive and, as we learned from the Mental Merry-Go-Round, will only give you more problems. On the other hand, solution thinking is Constructive and will give you more solutions. Problem thinkers are focused primarily on the problem and how bad it makes them feel. Solution thinkers concentrate on what caused the problem and how it can be avoided in the future. Solution thinkers are the ones who usually take charge of a situation because the problem thinkers are too busy feeling sorry for themselves.

> *"If you're not part of the solution, you're part of the problem."*
>
> AFRICAN PROVERB

AFFIRMATIONS DON'T WORK

I want be very clear about something: Solution thinking is *not* positive thinking. Positive thinking isn't always productive or helpful. In fact, positive thinking can actually frustrate you more and make the problem worse. Besides, how often do you feel like thinking happy, smiley thoughts when you're completely pissed off? A positive thinker who sees a pile of dirty dishes in the kitchen sink can close her eyes and say, "There are no dirty dishes, there are no dirty dishes." But when she opens her eyes those dishes will still be there and she'll still feel overwhelmed. Positive thinking and affirmations don't work because they don't focus your attention on solutions. They only give you false hope and empty wishes and neither is very satisfying or solves your problems.

"The pessimist complains about the wind;
the optimist expects it to change;
the realist adjusts the sails."

WILLIAM ARTHUR WARD

When you are solution thinking you are using the frustration, anger, sadness, guilt, fear, or whatever else you may be feeling to resolve the issue. You actually use the unpleasant emotion to help you resolve the issue. You may do this by deciding you never want to feel that way again. Or you may use the emotion as a springboard to become more determined to get what you want. By accepting the unpleasant emotions you open your mind to solutions.

On the other hand, if you're problem thinking, you're letting those unpleasant emotions use you. When you focus on and complain about your problem, you close your mind to any possible solutions and the frustration only grows. The old saying is true: What you resist persists. By asking, "What can I do differently next time?" or "This being the case how shall I proceed?" you are opening your mind to solutions.

When you're solution thinking, you actually use the unpleasant emotion to help you resolve the issue. Problem thinkers let their unpleasant feelings use them.

Problem thinking is also very draining. Have you ever dated a problem thinker, someone who constantly laments about his problems and how bad things are for him? Do you ever feel exhausted when you are with such a person? Negativity is energy taking. A problem thinker will take your energy and you will feel lethargic and tired. Solution thinkers are bundles of energy and are constantly giving energy to others. When you're around a solution thinker you'll notice how good you feel and how much energy you have.

Rather than focusing on the unwanted result and slipping into problem thinking, focus on what you want and practice solution thinking instead. Solution thinking will make good use of your frustration and will move you past whatever is causing you angst. Problem thinking only exacerbates the frustration and does nothing to resolve the issue.

EMOTIONAL vs. LOGICAL THINKING

Why do we have certain thoughts and why do we make certain choices even when we know it's not the best decision? A lot of what happens in the brain is based on what emotional benefit we gain from making a certain decision. It does this by comparing the present situation to similar situations from your past.

At the subconscious level your brain weighs the pros and cons of making a certain decision and anticipates how you will feel after deciding. The subconscious thinks, "If I act this way I will get this emotional benefit from it; I will feel more worthy and loved." This is why we keep acting the same way in the same situations and how Sore Spots are created. Your brain thinks, "Hmmm, what I did last time gave me attention." So it does it again because it knows it'll get attention just like it did before.

The brain can think emotionally, which is short-term, or logically, which can be short or long-term. Every brain is of two minds about the relationship. Your brain will do what it needs to in order to get attention and feel loved as soon as possible. It doesn't care about long-term consequences. It wants to feel better now. Emotional thinking and logical thinking compete against each other when the mind has to choose between short-term and long-term benefits.

Our emotional mind doesn't think about the future, while our logical mind clearly sees the future consequences of what we're doing. Think of it like this: Our emotional mind is on a continual shopping spree while our logical mind knows we should be saving for retirement.

"The heart has its reasons,
which reason knows nothing of."

BLAISE PASCAL

You feel conflicted because your logic is wrestling with your emotions. This is why it's crucial to notice long-term vs. short-term benefits. What we do may make us feel more worthy in the short-term, but in the long run it will make us feel less worthy. Yelling at your partner is a simple example. Long-term you feel ashamed and guilty, which is damaging to your self-esteem. You may get what you want and feel better initially, but over the long haul it will eat through the foundation of the relationship just like those termites.

Most people live their whole life like that. It's the downside of living in our current culture. We want everything instantly. We've got fast food, faster cars, eight-minute abs, one-minute managers, minute rice, instant oatmeal, high speed Internet, and we've even got speed dating. We're given a glimpse of how we'll feel if we do something and we don't stop to think what the long-term consequences will be. That's why we eat a quart of ice cream even though we want to lose 20 pounds. Logically we know eating ice cream will take us off our diet but emotionally we just want to feel better now. Emotion is always short-term. Logic can be both. The two things you can do to stop the cycle are, 1) be aware of what benefit you're getting from the short-term reward and determine how you can get that benefit long-term instead and, 2) use a pattern interrupt, which we'll discuss in chapter fifteen.

If we are unhappy and don't feel good about ourselves, we'll do something so we can feel good quickly. That's where we ignore the long-term and jump at the short-term reward. This contributes to the creation of Sore Spots.

A PENNY COMPOUNDED

Pretend I am the boss of a company and I have to leave for a month. Imagine I ask you to take over my job for the next thirty days. Although the job is only worth $4000, I will give you a choice of accepting $7000 up front or accepting payment at the end. Taking a penny on the first day and doubling the amount every day thereafter for thirty days determines the payment at the end. Quick, which offer would you accept?

Most people don't even hesitate. Their emotional thinking quickly takes the fast $7000. However, if given the opportunity, the logical mind will grab a calculator and quickly discover that the penny, compounded daily, is the wiser and more profitable decision to make. If you do the math you'll find that a penny, doubled every day will be worth $327.68 after 15 days. That's hardly worth the effort of driving to work. Continue for thirty days, however, and the total amounts to $10, 737,418.24. Did you get that? Over ten million dollars! Hmmm, now that may be worth waiting thirty days for.

"Only dead fish swim with the stream."

PROVERB

Sometimes you have to wait a little longer in order to get the payoff. Practice the guided imagery at the end of chapter thirteen and answer the questions in this book honestly and completely and the results you get will be priceless.

But sometimes we find ourselves in difficult situations and we have to respond and cope quickly so the mind makes the easiest and fastest choice that will make us feel worthy and loved. This behavior may be Constructive or Destructive. If it's Destructive and makes us feel worthy or loved it creates a Sore Spot.

KATHLEEN

Kathleen believes her husband, Gary, is cheating on her. Although her rational, logical mind can't find any evidence, her fantasizing, emotional mind continues to imagine the whole affair. Every detail is imagined. She knows the times, the places, and the stories he uses to cover it up. She sees the affair playing out in her mind again and again. In a jealous rage she confronts her husband. She is humiliated, angry, hurt, sad, and disgusted. In her mind it is the absolute truth. When he is confronted, Gary is shocked and denies everything. He is not having an affair. Despite his denials, she holds her position and swears she'll get even.

Even though he's not cheating, Kathleen believes it to be true. She has seen the images of him cheating in her mind so many times that it has become the absolute truth for her. Rationalizing with her will do little to appease her because she is caught up in her fantasy. Her emotional mind has won out over her logical mind.

If a child is afraid of the dark and thinks there's a ghost in his room, he's using his emotional thinking mind. Logical thinking isn't going to make him feel any better. Telling him logically there's no such thing as ghosts isn't going to be heard by him because he is emotionally thinking, which is short-term. You have to appeal to the child's emotional mind and tell him the ghost is actually his Guardian Angel who is there to protect him from the "bad" ghosts.

Think back to our two fears of not being worthy and not being loved. Our two fears are not logical. Logically, I can tell you we're all worthy of being loved. You *are* good enough and you *are* loved. But that little child inside you is thinking emotionally and remembers what it was like to be neglected, rejected, abused, ignored, or controlled. That's why looking back on our behavior it may seem that we acted irrationally. But at the time it really did make us feel better.

Have you ever argued with your partner and either he or you leaves before the issue is resolved? It could be hours later and there you are still arguing with him in your mind. He's already moved on to more important things while your emotional mind can't stop arguing with him. When we're focused on what we don't want, we're going to get more of what we don't want. So what's the difference between the person who keeps the argument going in her mind and the person who doesn't? The answer is your ability to focus on what you want.

Let's go back to the example of Kathleen, who believes Gary is cheating on her. Rather than explaining logically why

Kathleen is wrong, Gary would do better to appeal to her emotional mind. She needs to know she can *trust* him and feel less *neglected*. So he might tell her how much he misses her and how great it would be if she would call him every once in while when he is working late. This gives Kathleen a sense of control and let's her know she's not being excluded from his life. He could also mention how exhausted he is from working so late, but how it's going to be worth it when he uses some of the extra income to take her on a romantic getaway where they can re-connect on a more intimate level. By understanding what she's feeling, what her needs are, and what she's focused on, Gary is able to appeal to her emotional mind.

> *"You don't drown by falling in the water;*
> *you drown by staying there."*
> EDWIN LOUIS COLE

WHAT ARE YOU CARRYING?

There is an old story about two monks walking together and keeping each other company on their journey. At one point they came to a river that had no bridge. Realizing they had to cross it, they began taking off their shoes and rolling up their robes. Just then, a young woman approached and asked if one of the monks would carry her across the river so she could avoid getting wet. Both of the monks remembered the vow they had taken to never touch a woman. Honoring his vows the first monk politely refused. The second monk, however, took the woman in his arms and carried her across the river. Once on the other side the woman thanked the monk and went about her way.

The two monks continued in silence for a while when finally the first monk could stay silent no more. "You know, we're not supposed to touch women," he said. "Yes," the second monk replied. The first monk continued, "You took a vow never to touch a woman." Again, the second monk nodded and said, "Yes. That is true." "Then why," asked the first monk, "why did you pick that woman up and carry her across the river?" The second monk looked at the first monk and calmly responded, "I put her down two miles back, why are you still carrying her?"

Focusing on results you don't want will never change the result.

Be careful what you're focusing on. If you're dwelling on problems it will do you no good. Focusing on results you don't want will never change the result. You have to switch your focus to what you do want. That means changing the thoughts you're thinking toward solutions. The truth is you can't think of a solution without thinking of the problem. That's okay. Just don't focus on the unwanted result or problem because that will never help you find a solution. Use the problem to help find a solution. Solution thinking is productive and Constructive. Problem thinking is unproductive and Destructive.

Thoughts can be beliefs, attitudes, opinions, values, decisions, goals, ideas, or dreams. It is our beliefs that cause us to make certain decisions, have certain ideas, and set certain goals. So our beliefs will ultimately cause us to aim higher or lower, which definitely affects our relationships. For this reason, we'll focus next on our beliefs.

10

Is the Glass Slipper Half Full or Half Empty?

*"There are two kinds of people:
those who believe they can and those who believe
they can't. And they're both right."*

HENRY FORD

BELIEVE IT OR NOT

Have you ever noticed some people get in accidents and some never do? Some people always get traffic tickets while others never do. Some people are always sick while others are always healthy. Some people believe they lead a charmed life. Others believe they are cursed. They are all correct. How can that be? You are what you think and what you believe.

Sometimes we hold onto our beliefs no matter how obvious it is that they are Destructive. There is a story of a psychiatrist whose patient thought he was a corpse. In an effort to prove him wrong he asked his patient if corpses bleed. The man replied, of course, that corpses do not bleed. The psychiatrist then asked the man if he would take part in an experiment where all he would do was prick the man's finger. His patient complied. When the psychiatrist pricked the man's finger it started to bleed. At this point the man exclaimed, "I was wrong! Corpses do bleed." Sometimes we need to recognize that we are holding on to a belief that no longer serves us.

Beliefs are feelings of certainty. Beliefs are not facts. Facts are facts. Light travels at 186 thousand miles per second. That's a fact. The Earth is 92 million miles from the Sun. That's a fact. Facts are true for everybody. "I'm not good enough" is only a belief. It's not a fact. The beliefs we hold are not characteristics of reality itself but simply beliefs *about* reality. For instance, a woman finally meets the man she's been infatuated with but her mind suddenly freezes and she can't think of anything to say. This makes her feel like a loser. But even though she feels like a loser does it mean she *is* a loser? Hardly.

Our beliefs are real to each of us individually insofar as they create our reality but they are not universally true. Facts are universally true. Our beliefs are only real to us. Beliefs are only as real as we think they are or allow them to be. What we believe to be true creates our experience and, therefore, our reality.

Our beliefs are only as real
as we think they are or allow them to be.

If you believe you're a lovable person you will allow others to love you and you will love others freely. This *thought* will make you *feel* more loving which makes you *act* more loving and gives you loving responses or *results*. This is one reality. If, on the other hand, you believe you're not good enough you will seek the love of another to fill the void inside you. This reality will fill you with self-doubt and destroy your confidence. Both realities are determined by a single belief.

The *thought*, "Nobody loves me" leads to a *feeling*, such as sadness. The feeling of sadness leads to a *behavior* like staying home and sulking. Staying home leads to the *result* of being alone. Finally, being alone reinforces the original thought, "Nobody loves me." Whew! That's the Mental Merry-Go-Round.

Sunscreen can block the most intense sunlight. One degree can keep water from boiling. Likewise, a simple belief can keep you from having a better relationship.

THE PROOF IS IN THE PUDDING

In his fascinating book, *The Holographic Universe*, Michael Talbot discusses many examples of how beliefs affect reality. One such example is the person who has been diagnosed with Multiple Personality Disorder. Right now you're probably thinking, "I've dated guys with multiple personalities!" But true multiples are capable of making remarkable physiological changes that began with a simple belief. This occurs because the multiple who changes personalities *believes* he is that other personality.

For instance, a multiple can drink a whole bottle of whiskey yet turn instantly sober when he switches personalities. Multiples are capable of making other physiological changes, as well. Eye color can change and scars, tumors, diabetes, allergies, and epilepsy all come and go with different personalities. The belief the multiple has that he is controlled by another personality is so strong that it affects basic physiological processes.

> *"Reality is merely an illusion,*
> *albeit a very persistent one."*
> ALBERT EINSTEIN

Talbot mentions Stigmata as another example of how beliefs affect behavior. The stigmata phenomenon occurs when the wounds of Christ's crucifixion spontaneously appear on an individual with Christian beliefs. Modern day stigmatists all exhibit their wounds, which signify where Christ was nailed to the cross, in the same manner – through the hands. However, the Romans placed the nails through the wrists because they knew the hands could not hold the weight of the body. Yet all modern day stigmatists manifest wounds through the hands. Why? Because since the eighth century artists have depicted Christ having been nailed to the cross through his hands. Also, if their wounds came from the same source, such as the real wounds of Christ, the size, shape, and location would be identical for each stigmatist. This is not the case, however. Instead, there is inconsistency from stigmatist to stigmatist regarding these wounds. We can therefore determine their wounds do not come from one source but from many different sources, such as their own beliefs about the wounds Christ suffered. It is fascinating that a simple belief can spontaneously create a wound. It stands to reason that if the mind can instantaneously create a wound, then it can just as easily heal one.

GET YOUR PEANUTS, HERE!

Monkey trainers in Africa have an interesting way of catching monkeys. They drill a hole in a coconut big enough for the monkey to put his hand through. They attach a rope to the other end of the coconut. Then they place peanuts inside the coconut and wait behind a shrub. The monkey comes over, reaches inside and grabs the peanuts but is unable to remove his hand because his fist is too large to fit through the hole. Now, all the trainer has to do is pull the rope and the monkey, shrieking the whole way, will follow him to captivity. Why? The monkey simply won't let go of the peanuts at any cost. All he has to do is drop the peanuts and pull his hand out to get away. But he won't.

What peanuts are you holding onto that are leading you to or keeping you in captivity? Your peanuts may take the form of limiting beliefs, old relationships, painful memories, or ghosts of boyfriends past. Whatever form they take, now is the time to open your fist, drop the peanuts, and free yourself from captivity.

We are not always conscious of our beliefs. They may be so ingrained in our thoughts that we aren't even aware of them. But they are there and they are constantly determining our behavior and the results we're getting in our relationships. Some beliefs have been ingrained since childhood from what we heard from our parents. What did you hear about men growing up? Did you hear things like men are all pigs, all men want is sex, or men don't change? When you hear something enough you start to believe it even if it's not necessarily true. If you believe men are pigs what are you going to attract? Can you say oink, oink?

Remember the little girl that's told she's stupid? She will subconsciously put herself in situations that make her act and feel stupid so she stays in line with her subconscious belief. Likewise, someone who believes she's clumsy will subconsciously spill a drink on her dress or knock something off a table. This "clumsy" behavior will be consistent with her belief about herself. It could also be how she gets attention. Either way it becomes a self-fulfilling prophecy that continually gets reinforced. It's due to something called Cognitive Dissonance.

COGNITIVE DISSONANCE

Cognitions are pieces of knowledge. The knowledge may be about an emotion, a value, a goal, and so on. For instance, the knowledge that your hair is brown is a cognition; the knowledge that you want to be married is a cognition; the knowledge that you don't want to have children is a cognition. We can all hold multiple cognitions simultaneously. These bits of knowledge, called cognitions, form relationships with one another that will either be in line with each other (consonant) or out of sync (dissonant).

Two cognitions are dissonant when they are in opposition to each other. When two cognitions are in opposition to each other we experience a great deal of mental stress. Just as being deprived of food for several hours will cause you to devour food as soon as possible to avoid further discomfort, you will also immediately seek to reduce the unpleasant mental stress caused by dissonance.

By changing one of the cognitions to make it consistent with the other we are able to reduce the unpleasant stress we're experiencing. For example, cognitive dissonance occurs when we say one thing and do another.

Annette told everyone she knew that Wayne was her soul mate and she was going to marry him. However, a year later she got cold feet and broke off the relationship a month before the wedding.

In this instance, the first cognition is the knowledge of having told someone that she was going to marry Wayne. The second cognition is the knowledge of doing something completely different. Annette did not marry Wayne. If we tell someone we're going to do something we must follow through or risk being a liar in our friends' eyes.

This, however, is far better than telling *ourselves* that we will do something and failing to follow through. When this happens we become a liar in our own eyes and that is something that hurts our self-esteem more than anything else. Being perceived as a liar to her friends as well as to herself causes mental stress or dissonance. There is dissonance because Annette knows she's not a liar, yet she also knows that she did not do what she said she would and is now perceived as a liar. This dissonance can be so uncomfortable for Annette that she will take action to alleviate it as soon as possible. The action she takes is changing one of the cognitions.

In other words, she will create a story that will reduce the dissonance and increase the consonance and get things back in sync. Her story will explain why she told the lie thereby exonerating her and reducing the cognitive dissonance. She will find it exceedingly difficult to live with herself if she perceives herself as dishonest and a liar. Creating a story, believing it, and sticking to it is a subconscious process designed to avoid cognitive dissonance and protect our fragile self-image.

When Annette says she broke it off because Wayne was too lazy and didn't earn enough to support a potential family, she begins to believe it even though Wayne is on the fast track to upper management in his computer software company. She had to come up with something to get her cognitions back in sync, and she will most likely believe this story until the day she dies.

What about that girl who was told she's stupid? The girl will experience cognitive dissonance if she does something brilliant because it goes against her belief of being stupid. When someone compliments her she will be conflicted with the two bits of knowledge that she is stupid but did something brilliant. To ease her mental anguish she may attribute the moment of brilliance to "dumb luck" or give credit to someone else altogether.

"You will resemble tomorrow the dominating thoughts that you keep alive in your mind today."

NAPOLEON HILL

TUG OF WAR

In this way a limiting belief or thought is a lot like a rope tied around your waist that keeps you tethered to where you are right now. Every time you see something you want and move toward it you only get so far before the rope yanks you back and keeps you from getting what you want. You may start a great relationship with a wonderful guy and just when things seem like they couldn't get any better, you're yanked back by a limiting belief.

This limiting belief may be something like, "I don't deserve to be happy." This belief hammers away until the relationship starts to fall apart. You don't notice the limiting belief because it's subconscious. It's become a habitual thought outside of your awareness and it's been strengthening that nerve cell connection for years without your knowing about it.

From what we've learned so far, it's easy to see how every thought, decision, and behavior you've ever had have led you to where you are right now. It's also easy to see how changing your thoughts, beliefs, and decisions will change your relationships. You have held some of these thoughts and beliefs since you were too young to remember. So, you may be uncomfortable with some of the information contained in these pages. That is by design. When you are uncomfortable with something, it means your beliefs, values, or attitudes are being challenged. When you are challenged, you have two choices: You can either give up or you can learn from it and evolve. We discover more about ourselves through troubled times than we do from cheerful times.

We discover more about ourselves through troubled times than we do from joyous times.

IT'S ALL MESSED UP

A mother sitting with her young daughter in front of her doll collection might take a doll out, play with it and set it back down. Her daughter, a bit miffed, may snort and hastily put the doll back in its "rightful" place. If the mother then took another doll and moved it to a different spot her frustrated daughter might snarl and say, "Mommy! Stop messing everything up." Is everything really messed up? Or is she frustrated because she has so many ways for things to be wrong and only one way for things to be right? The daughter is engaged in problem thinking, which focuses on what's wrong and how bad it makes her feel. If she were to make a simple shift to solution thinking she would be focused on what's right about the situation and she would feel better.

For instance, a woman may go into a relationship with certain limiting beliefs. She may believe that the only way for success is if he asks her to marry him. Her life will be pretty messed up if he doesn't even ask her for a second date. The woman who understands that a relationship is a chance to learn and evolve will live in a happier, more satisfying, and right world. She knows that if the relationship doesn't work out, she is still worthy of love and attention. She knows that what she has learned from this relationship will help her to form a stronger relationship in the future. She also understands that, contrary to the romantic idea of love, there is more than one person for her on this planet. She is comforted by the knowledge that she is now free to pursue somebody who will be a better fit for her. Best of all, she can now use the knowledge she gained from this relationship to better define the kind of partner she is looking for the next time around.

If she has many ways for the relationship to go right, even when it is ending, and only one or no way for the relationship to go wrong, she will be more empowered in her relationships. She will also enjoy dating much more than the person whose world is always messed up. This messed up person will only have one way, if any, for the relationship to be right and many ways for it to be wrong. She will never be satisfied and each subsequent relationship will be more devastating for her than the last. Eventually, convinced that she will never find the right guy, she will either be alone or settle for someone that truly is not right for her.

You are in charge of what you think about and how often you think about it.

As you have probably experienced, thoughts can be positive, negative, bizarre, or seem completely foreign to you. Strangely, when this happens most people assume that the thoughts are out of their control. They are much like the idle roommate who is too lazy to find the remote control, so he watches whatever is on that station.

Like the lazy roommate, most people relegate themselves to thinking whatever thoughts come to them with no clue whatsoever that they are completely capable of changing these thoughts at any time. Just as we change the channel when we don't like what we're watching, we can change the thoughts in our mind when we don't like what we're thinking. Just point the remote control and click. You are in charge of what you think about and how often you think about it.

> *"Men are not prisoners of fate,*
> *but only prisoners of their own minds."*
> FRANKLIN D. ROOSEVELT

It is the sum total of all your thoughts and decisions from the moment you were born until now that have put you where you are today. If you don't like where you are, you must change your thoughts and decisions. You must make the shift from problem thinking to solution thinking. When you are problem thinking you are focused on the problem and all it's negative side effects like feeling frustrated, depressed, or angry. Focusing on solutions will produce positive side effects like feeling energized and getting the results you want. Which do you prefer?

In order to move toward the relationship you want, you have to become aware of the thoughts that have been holding you back. You can recognize a problem thought quite easily once you know what to look for. You might say, "I'm going to find a great guy to date," and then that little voice inside says, "But you never could find one before." The problem thought will cancel out your Constructive intention and you will end up frustrated. That's cognitive dissonance and it's precisely why you must become aware of your Destructive, problem thinking. Once you're aware of this thought pattern you can change to more Constructive, solution thinking.

NEGATIONS

In order to change a problem thought, it's important to learn how to recognize one. There are a number of ways to recognize a problem thought. The first is being aware of negations. Examples of negations are negative words like "can't," "don't," "won't," "never," and "didn't." Pay attention to the things you say to yourself like, "I'm *not* good enough." Then immediately ask yourself, "What if I were good enough? What would happen if I were good enough?" If you find yourself thinking, "I *don't* have time for a relationship," ask yourself, "What if I *did* have time? How *can* I make time?" Counter the thought, "I'll *never* find my soul mate" with questions such as, "Never? What would happen if I *did*?" You'll be amazed at how simple it is to switch from problem to solution thinking.

DEMANDS

We place demands on ourselves in order to live up to the expectations of others as well as ourselves. We are demanding when we use words like "should," "shouldn't," "have to," and "must." Using words like these limits our choices and relinquishes our power. We put undo pressure on ourselves by saying to ourselves, "I *have to* find a date this weekend" or "I *should* be married by now." Such all or nothing statements cause anxiety and set us up for failure. To paraphrase psychologist Fritz Perls, most people think they *should* do this or they *should* do that. But in the end all they ever do is "should" all over themselves.

When you find yourself using negations or demands you can regain control over your thoughts by using words such as "choose to," "want to," and "choose not to." For example, "I shouldn't go" is limiting whereas, "I'm choosing to stay home" keeps you in charge of the decisions you make. More importantly, you stop 'should-ing' on yourself.

COMPARISONS

Any time you compare yourself to someone or something you are problem thinking. Examples of comparisons are, "I'm too emotional," "I'm too heavy," "I'm not good enough," "She's prettier," "I'm not worthy" or "I'm too old." When you find yourself making comparison remarks immediately ask yourself, "Too heavy compared to what?" "Not worthy compared to whom?" "Who says she's prettier?" We all have our own unique qualities and each of us has our own road to travel. To compare yourself to another person only limits you from achieving what you want in your relationship. Besides, if each of us is truly unique and there is no other person on the planet like us, then precisely with whom are we comparing ourselves?

THE PROCESS OF FEELING "NOT"

Anything you cannot feel is a problem thought. For instance, "I'm not happy." How does one feel "not?" I can feel happy. I can feel sad or angry or even guilty. However, it is impossible to feel "not." By saying "I don't feel happy" you're denying your true feelings and limiting your experience, which, in turn, limits what you need to learn from that particular situation. If you don't learn what you need to from that event you will continue to make the same mistake until you do learn your lesson. When you find yourself thinking something like this ask yourself, "If I *don't* feel happy then what *do* I feel?" The answer may surprise you.

PROBLEM THOUGHT	*SOLUTION THOUGHT*
"I don't know."	*"What if I did know?"*
"I can't do that."	*"If I <u>can't</u> do that, what <u>can</u> I do?"*
"I won't do that."	*"If I <u>won't</u> do that, what <u>will</u> I do?"*
"I can't afford it."	*"What do I have to do so I <u>can</u> afford it?" or "How <u>can</u> I afford it?"*
"I'm not good enough."	*"What if I were?"*
"She's prettier than me."	*"Says who?" "Compared to whom?"*
"It doesn't ___."	*"If it doesn't ___, what does ___?"*
"I couldn't ___."	*"What if I could ___?"*
"I wouldn't ___."	*"What if I would ___?" or "What would happen if I did?"*

I trust you get the idea. Instead of narrowing your mind to problems by thinking things like, "I can't" or "I don't know," switch your thoughts to solutions by asking yourself the opposite of each statement or thought. By doing this you will open your mind to solutions for any problem.

Now it's your turn. Make a list of at least ten "problem" thoughts you have and write their "solution" thought alternatives.

PROBLEM THOUGHT   **SOLUTION THOUGHT**

_____   _____

_____   _____

_____   _____

_____   _____

_____   _____

By taking charge of your thoughts you can switch your focus to what you want rather than what you don't want. It is noticing Destructive or problem thinking and changing it to Constructive or solution thinking. By changing your _thought_ you focus on what you want. Focusing on what you want will make you _feel_ good. Feeling good makes you _behave_ Constructively. Constructive behavior produces positive _results_ for you. Those positive results turn right around and reward you by reinforcing your solution thinking. And so it goes on the Mental Merry-Go-Round.

When we're unaware of our thoughts we are at their mercy. By being unaware of what we're thinking from moment to moment we are playing a game of chance, hoping against hope that the odds are with us. The truth is the odds are against you. We've already learned that about eighty percent of our thoughts are negative. That means you've got a very small chance of getting the results you want. Those odds increase in your favor when you pay attention to what you're thinking and take charge of your thoughts, beliefs, decisions, goals, and so on.

When we're unaware of our thoughts we are at their mercy.

Changing a thought creates and reinforces the nerve cell connection that was created when the thought was originally produced. When you think that thought again it strengthens that connection making it harder to not think that thought. It also makes it more difficult to think that problem thought again. Soon this new way of thinking becomes a habit and you're continually focused on what you want. Eventually all this habitual solution thinking produces the results you want and you enjoy the Mental Merry-Go-Round more than ever. Once you've mastered the Mental Merry-Go-Round you'll be more aware of the people who get sick on the ride, the problem thinkers, and you'll gravitate more toward those who enjoy the ride, the solution thinkers.

"You can't stop the waves from coming, but you can learn to surf."
SWAMI SATCHIDANANDA

Now, are you always going to enjoy the ride? No. Let's face it, there will be times when things are getting rotten and you just feel like screaming. By all means scream. Keeping it all inside and putting a shiny spin on everything is nearly impossible and could even compromise your health. Sometimes we just want to bitch about something. Go for it!

Even a monk has a bad day once in a while. Once you're through venting, get your mind back on the solution track. Bad moods are only a problem if they persist. If you're into your second or third day of a bad mood, it's time to do something about your problem thoughts. You can't stop thoughts from coming. But you can determine where those thoughts take you.

You don't have to do it all at once. Ease into your new way of thinking. Your goal is to be solution thinking about twenty percent of the time by the end of the first week. Forty percent of all your thoughts the second week should be solution based. The next week, aim for seventy percent. By the end of the fourth week you will be an expert at solution thinking.

> ### *When you change your beliefs*
> ### *you change your world.*

SPARE SOME CHANGE?

It is entirely possible to change your thoughts and beliefs. We do it every day without thinking about it. In one study, researchers went to the racetrack and surveyed people before and after they placed their bets. They discovered only sixty percent of the people believed they would win before placing their bet. However, after they placed the bet a full ninety-five percent believed they would win.

Something similar occurs when you buy something, like a computer. If, prior to making your purchase, you were asked which is the best computer out there, you may be unsure. Once you bought the computer, however, you would say that the one in your possession is the best. After all, why would you buy it if it weren't the best? Why on earth would you keep dating him if he weren't a good boyfriend?

How do these belief shifts occur? Once we get committed and take action we change our beliefs to support our actions. We convince ourselves that we must like him more than we thought otherwise we wouldn't be dating him. We do this to avoid cognitive dissonance and looking like a liar to our loved ones and ourselves.

When some hot guy walks into the restaurant you might believe he is out of your league. After you notice him smiling and glancing your way you may believe that the two of you might be soul mates. It makes no difference what kind of beliefs they are. We change our beliefs every day without even thinking about it. By unlearning what is giving you the results you don't want, you will be able to learn how to produce the results you do want.

Remember, beliefs aren't facts; they are only feelings of certainty. People used to believe the world was flat. They were one hundred percent certain that if they wandered too far from home they might fall off the edge of the earth. Then one day, a guy named Columbus went out and sailed around the world. He came back and proclaimed the world to be, in fact, round. When you change your beliefs you change your world.

11

The Illusion Of Reality

"Man is what he believes."

ANTON CHEKHOV

I BELIEVE IT SO IT MUST BE TRUE

In her book, *The Myth Of Repressed Memory: False Memories And Allegations Of Sexual Abuse,* Dr. Elizabeth Loftus demonstrates that continually thinking about something will eventually cause you to believe it. Loftus conducted a study in which researchers implanted a false memory into the minds of their subjects. The content of the made-up memory was that of being lost in the shopping mall as a child. The researchers only had to say things like, "Try and remember" or, "Think about it. Do you remember any details at all?" Soon the subjects did recall the incident. Even more surprising, not only did they believe it, they added facts and details to the false memory that never occurred.

"Remember, Jerry, it's not a lie if you believe it."

GEORGE COSTANZA
SEINFELD

The fact that the subjects expanded on the memory and added facts that were suggested by the researchers means the false memory became very real to the subject. Even more interesting, when informed weeks later that the memory was false, the subjects vehemently argued that they were, in fact, lost in the mall as a child. When you think about something enough, even if it's not true, it becomes real to you.

This is why the woman who thinks her husband is having an affair believes beyond a shadow of a doubt he's cheating. You and I, and her husband in particular, will have a hard time convincing her otherwise. She has thought about it so much, and continually added details and facts to the false memories, that they are just as true for her as the sun coming up in the morning.

Have you ever thought your boyfriend forgot your birthday and you got so angry and hurt you felt the relationship was beyond repair? What happened when you discovered he didn't forget but instead planned a surprise romantic getaway weekend? Did you feel embarrassed? Silly? It was real for you because you told yourself he forgot and in your mind that meant he didn't care about you. In your emotional mind you saw him goofing around with his friends or watching TV instead of shopping for your birthday gift. It became real to you and you were upset because of it. But it wasn't true. It's important to understand the difference between a belief and a fact.

"If you have negative feelings about something you will attract those feelings like a magnet."

CARL JUNG

BIRDS OF A FEATHER FLOCK TOGETHER

There is a law of the Universe called the Law of Attraction. It says that like attracts like. We see this every day. Loud people attract loud people. Quiet people attract quiet people. Insecure people attract insecure people. Moreover, if you have negative feelings about something, you will attract those negative feelings like a magnet. So a fear of dogs attracts more dogs. If you dislike immature men, you'll bump into immature men on every corner.

What you put out will always come back to you.

Why? Simply put, the Law of Attraction means "birds of a feather flock together." Those birds can be thoughts, feelings, or behaviors. Of course we know that thoughts, feelings, and behaviors give us results and those results will flock together too. You get what you focus on or what you think about so what you put out will come back to you. The Law of Attraction is the fundamental rule for the Mental Merry-Go-Round.

"We make a living by what we get.
We make a life by what we give."
SIR WINSTON CHURCHILL

If you ping a tuning fork in a room full of tuning forks, all the other forks tuned to the same frequency will begin to ping without even touching them. This same principle applies to us. Negative people hang around negative people, and they hate positive people. Insecure people hang around insecure people. Happy people hang around happy people. Miserable people can't stand being around happy people. If you have low self-esteem, you'll attract someone with low self-esteem.

Have you ever seen a chameleon sitting on a rock and watched as it assumed the color of that rock? The human mind is like that chameleon. We become what we're thinking about. If our mind is focused on gossip, worries, hatred, loneliness, and so on, it will assume those qualities. If you think about joy, peace, love, companionship, or romance you will become just that. Our thoughts create our reality. By focusing on love, happiness, and fulfillment we create love, happiness, and fulfillment in our relationships.

We become what we think about.

Let me give you an example of how two people with similar beliefs will attract each other. Jessica's boyfriend Todd is physically and verbally abusive toward her. Why is she abused? Maybe she holds the beliefs that men are dangerous, aggressive, and can't be trusted and that she's not worthy of being with a respectful man. By holding these beliefs in her mind Jessica attracts exactly what she believes. She responds to her beliefs by becoming the victim in the relationship.

"We will not attract what we are not."
CARL JUNG

Todd holds similar beliefs. He believes men are strong, aggressive, and don't have to respect women because women are weak and are here only to serve his needs. He acts on his beliefs by lying, cheating, beating her, and calling her stupid and worthless. Both hold similar beliefs so they attract each other yet each acts on their beliefs differently. One acts as the victim and the other as the aggressor but they both need each other in order for their beliefs to hold true.

If you are strong and controlling and attract and date only weak or submissive men, you are reinforcing each other's beliefs. You appear stronger when compared to him, while he appears weaker compared to you. Being with each other is continually supporting your beliefs. Would your belief be supported if you dated aggressive and abusive men? You wouldn't look or feel very strong if you did, would you?

116

Likewise, your weak boyfriend wouldn't know how to respond if his girlfriend was weaker than him. His identity would be lost and he would be confused and anxious.

Remember, what you think about will strengthen the nerve cell connection that was created the first moment you had that thought and reinforced every time after that. If you stop thinking that thought you will sever the connection.

WHEN IT RAINS IT POURS

Not only do you get what you're focused on, according to the second law of the Universe, the Law of Abundance, you get *more* of whatever you're focused on. Remember, the Law of Attraction says what you put out comes back to you. But the Law of Abundance says not only does it come back to you, it comes back in greater number and in different forms. This is why someone who's a negative or problem thinker not only gets more of the problem she's thinking about, she also gets other problems like arguments, getting dumped, being cheated on, ignored, stood up, or rejected. In her life she may get in accidents, get tickets, get robbed, have her computer crash, get fired, get cut off on the highway, or evicted from her apartment. She has all this bad stuff happen because she's coming from a bad place in her thoughts and until she switches her focus, the Mental Merry-Go-Round will continue to produce bad stuff in her relationships as well as in her life.

On the other hand, the woman who is a solution thinker will get more solutions and positive experiences from her relationship. She'll get better boyfriends, more romance, deeper connection, and more passion. In her life she will attract things like more money, better job opportunities, a safe neighborhood to live in, discounted vacations, and so on. We can sum up the Law of Abundance with one phrase: "When it rains it pours." Going back to problem versus solution thinking, if you problem think you're going to get more rain and storm clouds. You're going to get more problems. If you begin to think solutions you will get more sun and blue sky. You're going to get more solutions. The Law of Attraction and the Law of Abundance say what you put out will come back to you, and when it comes back it will be even stronger and in greater number. So be careful what you're putting out there. You just might get it.

12

The Way We Word

*"Words form the thread on which we
string our experiences."*

ALDOUS HUXLEY

STICKS AND STONES

An easy way to focus on what you want is to become aware of the words you use to describe what's going on in your relationship. The old nursery rhyme "sticks and stones may break my bones but words will never hurt me" isn't entirely true.

In fact, recent research has shown that a social snub affects the brain exactly the way physical pain does. According to Matt Lieberman, a social psychologist at UCLA, when you get your feelings hurt, it really hurts you. In other words, there's no difference between physical pain and social pain. The words we use to label the experience of a snub, for example, cause us to feel physical pain. If we say, "It felt like I got socked in the gut when he dumped me" we may actually feel a pit in our stomach. Since every thought you have gets communicated to every cell in your body, when someone "breaks your heart" it's not too far from the truth.

The words we use have an enormous impact on our relationships. Think about it. If he leaves the toilet seat up and you say, "That jerk!" you're going to feel differently toward him than if you had said, "I guess he just forgot." The thought leads to the feeling. The feeling leads to a behavior and that behavior creates a result. Always. Every time. Furthermore, that result is now reinforcing that thought and strengthening that nerve connection making it harder to not think that thought or feel that feeling or act that way. It becomes harder to not get that result. The Mental Merry-Go-Round never stops.

> *The thought leads to the feeling. The feeling leads to a behavior and that behavior creates a result. Always. Every time.*

The words we use to label our experiences affect how we feel about something and how we'll respond to it. Human beings created language so we could express ourselves and communicate more clearly. Language attaches meaning to our experiences and every word has a different meaning for each of us. For instance, if I say the word "man" who are you thinking of? Are you thinking of the guy that sold me my car? Even though I was thinking of the guy who sold me my car I'll bet you weren't thinking of him. If you were it would be creepy.

You may have been thinking about your boyfriend, father, friend, a celebrity, or maybe you did the opposite and thought of a woman. Perhaps you saw the word 'man' in your mind. We all think of different things because the word 'man' means something different to each of us. In fact, every word has a different meaning for each of us. If you ask six billion people on this planet to define the meaning of love, you will get six billion different definitions.

Think about two words that imply being alone, yet give vastly different meanings to our situation. If we're *lonely,* we're miserable. But if we experience *solitude,* we become the envy of friends and coworkers who wish they could have some peace and quiet too.

From meaning or thought comes emotion. You get a much different feeling when you say, "Oops" as opposed to, "I'm so stupid." If you've ever seen a drop of gasoline in water you know that a single drop of gasoline will spread over the water instantly. The words we use spread across and influence our relationships just as quickly.

If you change the word, you change the meaning. When you change the meaning, you change the feeling. By changing the feeling, you change the behavior. Changing the behavior lets you change the result. And round and round we go on The Mental Merry-Go-Round.

Be aware of the words you use to describe how you feel or how you express an emotion directly. Once you are aware of these words, change them to make the positive feelings more compelling or the unpleasant emotions less severe or important. Play with the words and notice which ones feel better to you. Change "depressed" to "uncomfortable;" "happy" to "ecstatic;" "fine" to "excellent;" "angry" to "disappointed." The sooner you switch your words, the faster you'll begin to feel better, and the more quickly your relationship will get better.

A wife who is constantly told she is stupid by her husband will eventually believe she really is stupid. Likewise, if we make a mistake and say to ourselves, "That was dumb" or "I'm an idiot" we begin to accept it as truth. If we say it or hear it over and over we'll eventually believe it. It becomes a self-fulfilling prophecy. Pay attention to the words you use.

HOW ARE YOU?

For instance, what do you say when someone asks, "How are you today?" Most people will say something like, "fine" or "okay" or "I'm all right." Worse yet, some people will launch into a story about how bad their life is and what a rotten day they're having and on and on and on they go until you're sorry you ever asked. But what would happen if you were to say, "I'm excellent" or "outstanding" or "great?" By saying, "excellent" or another positive and empowering alternative, you actually send the message to your body that you really are excellent.

Remember, every thought you have gets directly communicated to every cell in your body. When your body hears the word 'excellent' it believes it is excellent. Not only will you begin to feel better but you'll make someone else's day, too.

Try it the next time you're at the grocery store. When the check out clerk slides your peanut butter through the scanner and without looking at you asks, "How are you?" respond by saying, "I'm excellent, how are you?" Then, just sit back and notice his response. Nine times out of ten the checker will stop what he's doing, look at you and say, "Excellent? Wow, you must be having a pretty good day." You will actually see a physiological shift occur inside the checker as he stands a little more upright and smiles. It is so easy to make yourself feel better and to brighten someone else's day as well.

THE BUTCHER'S LESSON

According to an old Zen story, a man was walking through a market when he overheard a customer tell the butcher, "I would like the very best cut of meat you have." The butcher replied, "Every cut of meat in my shop is the finest. There isn't one cut here that's not the best." In other words, the butcher was saying that whatever you're looking for is exactly what you'll find.

If you're looking for the flaws in your partner, you'll find many. If you're looking for why he's so wonderful, you'll find many of those too. You could ask ten different people in the butcher shop and you'll get ten different responses as to which is the best cut of meat.

Have you ever noticed how friends and family often see the wonderful qualities in your partners but you only see the ones that annoy you? You're so focused on what you don't like about him that you can't see what you do like about him. Or you may have done the opposite. You ignore the red flags, even though your friends and family are constantly pointing them out.

When we have a problem and we ask ourselves, "What's *wrong* with me" what are we going to find? We're going to find all kinds of stuff in our past that supports what's wrong with us because that's what we're looking for. Your internal search engine will find things that are wrong with you. But what would happen if you were to ask, "What's *right* with me?" What will you find when you go back into your past? That's right. You'll find all kinds of wonderful things that support what's right with you. Your brain will rewire itself making it easier to find things that are right with you. This principle applies directly to your relationship. When you ask yourself, "What's wrong with him," what are you going to find? And what will you find when you ask yourself, "What's right with him?" Now you've got it.

This works out loud, as well. If you compliment him frequently you'll discover that you're more attracted to him. You'll be less attracted to him if you tell him he's late, he forgot to take out the trash, he left the toilet seat up, or he watches too much TV. The more you say it, the more you believe it. Your subconscious thinks, "I must love him because I keep complimenting him." By keeping your thoughts in sync, your mind avoids that dreaded cognitive dissonance. It works the other way, as well. Your subconscious mind might be thinking, "I must not like him very much because all I do is bitch about all the things he's doing wrong." What quality of meat are you looking for?

13

Journey Back To You

*"No one can make you feel inferior
without your consent."*

ELEANOR ROOSEVELT

What role does self-esteem play in our relationships? If we
have low self-esteem then every time we say, "I love you"
what we really mean is, "I don't think about my lousy
childhood when I'm with you and I will continue to love you
as long as you make me feel this way. The moment you
don't make me feel better, I won't love you anymore and I
will look for someone else who does."

Our partners can't fix whatever it is that caused our self-
esteem to bottom out. Yet we look to Prince Charming as if
just being around him will be enough to raise our self-worth.
We think all we need is that glass slipper and everything will
be miraculously better.

The truth is if you don't love yourself, you are incapable of
loving someone else. And while it may feel great in the
beginning of the relationship, eventually reality is going to
set in and you're going to be reminded that you're not good
enough. If you can recognize these moments and take charge
of them, you will be halfway to higher self-esteem.

When we feel a little insecure, it's a message from our mind warning us that we don't totally believe we have the ability to succeed in the current situation. We don't feel we're good enough to make the right choices and we don't deserve to be happy. We feel trepidation when we stand amongst the "grown-ups" so we become the small child who never belonged, felt loved, or had a sense of control over her environment or herself.

> *"You have no idea what a poor opinion*
> *I have of myself and how little I deserve it."*
>
> W.S. GILBERT

THREE'S COMPANY

Low self-esteem can get us into relationships that aren't exactly what we expected. If you do not have the relationship you always thought you'd have, it's because you're stuck in one of the following three categories:

1. Lack of Definition

2. Lack of Action

3. Lack of Belief

We'll focus primarily on the lack of belief since without the belief you cannot clearly define what you want or take action to get it. We already know a belief is a thought that sets in motion the Mental Merry-Go-Round. Furthermore, a lack of belief in our ability to have a better relationship can be traced directly to the level of our self-esteem. Until you are in charge of all three categories you will not experience the kind of relationship you desire.

LACK OF DEFINITION

Hazy and vague goals produce hazy and vague results. Someone suffering from low self-esteem cannot define her ideal mate because she has no clearly defined Self. How can I define what I want if I don't even know who I am? If you don't know who you are you couldn't possibly have a clear idea of what your ideal relationship would be. As a result, you may rely on what others tell you or what movies, television, and magazines say is the "ideal" relationship. Just as one diet doesn't work for each of us, the same ideal won't satisfy everyone. One size does not fit all. In fact we each have our own definition of love, the ideal mate, and the perfect relationship. All we have to do is search deep enough to find it. In order to have the relationship you want, you must clearly define what your ideal relationship is. In order to do that you must have a clearly defined Self.

"A lot of my life happened in great, wonderful bursts of good fortune, and then I would race to be worthy of it."

JULIE ANDREWS

LACK OF ACTION

Many times we don't take action to get what we want because we don't believe we're good enough to have it. We don't give one hundred percent when we don't feel one hundred percent. Even if he looks and acts like the man of your dreams, if you don't feel worthy of his attention you won't approach him or send out signals for him to approach you.

If you're single, you may not be doing what it takes to meet your ideal mate or to have a healthy, fulfilling relationship. For instance, you have to go where your ideal man might be in order to meet him. If you're looking for an Italian arm wrestling champion you have to go where Italian arm wrestling champions hang out. Don't go to rave parties expecting to find a bunch of CEO's. You don't look for water in the desert. Go where your type of guy hangs out.

If you're in a relationship, a lack of action may take the form of not communicating clearly, effectively, or respectfully all of your wants, needs, and desires. A lack of action may also include avoiding resolving your issues through clear communication, compromise, and cooperation. You may not be taking action to resolve differences because you believe he is the one who needs to take the action since he's the one with the problem. Can you say Sore Spot?

LACK OF BELIEF

Lack of belief is the most important of the three categories of reasons for not having the relationship you want. If I don't believe I'm worthy, I won't believe I deserve a better relationship or that my ideal mate would even want me. I won't take the time to define what I'm looking for and I won't do what is necessary to have the relationship I want because of the lack of belief in myself. There are three primary beliefs you need to possess in order to experience your idea of the perfect relationship:

1. Believe you *want* to have a better relationship.

2. Believe you *can* have a better relationship.

3. Believe you are *worthy* of having a better relationship.

If you don't possess all three of these beliefs you will not get more out of your relationship. You'll get less. If you don't believe you *can* have a better relationship, you're not going to try. If you don't believe you're *worthy* of a better relationship, you're going to settle for less. If you don't believe you *want* a better relationship, then you're probably getting some emotional benefit from playing the victim in a bad relationship.

These beliefs operate at the subconscious level and are forged at an early age from observing our parents. Becoming aware of them, therefore, is paramount if you want to heal your Sore Spot and experience a better relationship.

THE "I'M O.K. CORRAL"

Self-esteem is developed from birth and is defined as:

1. Having confidence that you can face and cope with life's challenges.

2. Knowing you're worthy of being happy.

Healthy self-esteem is having high regard for your Self while low self-esteem is just the opposite. In short, self-esteem is how worthy you feel in any given situation. Individuals who have low self-esteem only value themselves if certain conditions are met, like having a date on Saturday night, for instance. This spills over to their relationships. People with low self-esteem will often put conditions on their love. If their partner does not comply, they withdraw their love. People with high self-esteem do not put conditions on their love for themselves or others.

According to researcher Stanley Coopersmith, when it comes to self-esteem, wealth, education, where you live, parents' occupation, and having a stay at home Mom don't matter. There are four things that do matter:

1. **The child feels her thoughts and feelings are unconditionally accepted and valued.** This means no matter how the child feels, whether it's angry, frustrated, elated, indifferent, or sad, the child is nurtured and supported.

2. **Reasonable rules are set and enforced.** Parents explain rules and allow the child to discuss the rules with them.

3. **The parents do not control the child with violence (threatened or real) or humiliation.** The child is given reasonable levels of demands and reasons for the demands.

4. **The parents have healthy self-esteem themselves.** This means they don't try to boost their self-esteem at the expense of the child by controlling, belittling, abusing, or criticizing. It also means they model appropriate behavior for the child.

How many of these did you experience as a child? Looking at this list, it's easy to see the quality of the relationship between the child and her parents is what matters most. Self-esteem develops from our own perception of ourselves. We get this perception from what we saw, heard, and experienced from our parents. We then generalize these perceptions to every relationship we have for the rest of our lives. This is how self-esteem affects our relationships as adults.

> *"Marriage is the nearest adult equivalent to the original parent-child relationship."*
>
> H.V. DICKS

When we're in a relationship, our inner child begins reliving our past so it can heal what was hurt inside of us. Every relationship we have serves to bring out issues we need to resolve as well as reinforce and validate our self-esteem. The problem is if we don't take time to resolve our past, no current relationship will be able to help our self-esteem. When we become aware of past issues and resolve them we allow ourselves to fully love our partner. Until then we are only pretending. We're only playing a game and hoping our partner can "save" us or make us whole again. This is a false hope that can result in feeling less worthy and unloved.

If we have low self-esteem and we attempt to feel more worthy and loved through Destructive or inappropriate behaviors, those behaviors will ultimately reinforce our low self-esteem. So it goes on the Mental Merry-Go-Round.

People with high self-esteem do not put conditions on their love for themselves or others.

INSIDE OUT

If you ask one hundred people, "Who are you?" you will hear things like, "I'm a doctor," "I'm a mother," or "I'm a chef." But that's not who they are, that's what they do. Our jobs, roles, responsibilities, cars, houses, and bank accounts do not define us. We are defined by who we are inside. Who we are inside is determined a great deal by our childhood experiences, how we dealt with them, and what we learned from them.

There are three ways in which self-esteem affects us:

1. **What's going on inside of us will filter everything we see outside of us.** When someone is depressed she believes she is depressed every minute of the day. She believes she never gets a break from feeling depressed. However, if you were to follow her around with a video camera, at some point you would capture her laughing, smiling, and enjoying a conversation with coworkers or friends. At the end of the day, if you asked her how her day was, she would tell you it was terrible because she was depressed all day long.

   If you were to play the video of her actually having fun during the day she may be surprised. This is because she remembers the day differently. At the subconscious level she chooses to remember only the times she was depressed. When she looks back on her day, she will see it from the viewpoint of a depressed person. Everything she experiences will first go through her depression filter. This viewpoint will bias her memory because she will attach depression to each memory. She becomes so focused on her depression and how bad it makes her feel that she fails to notice the times she isn't depressed.

Likewise, the person who filters everything through low self-esteem will not notice the opportunities that would give her more confidence. She won't notice the attractive man flirting with her. Instead, she believes he's just being nice because he feels sorry for her. Even though it's brilliant, she won't tell the boss about her idea because she doesn't believe she has anything to say that anyone wants to hear. It may be perfectly obvious to you and me, but she won't see it because of her low self-esteem filter.

2. **If you don't love yourself, you will allow others to control you in the relationship.** Subconsciously we're thinking things like, "I'll give him control so he won't leave me" and "He's better than me and I don't deserve him. Who am I to make decisions or demands anyway? I'm lucky just to have someone around." Low self-esteem will keep you in unhealthy relationships because you won't think you can do any better.

3. **A lack of Self leads to identifying with problems.** The subconscious thought pattern may go something like this: If I don't know who I am, if I have no clearly defined Self, then I won't get the attention I need. So I'd better identify with something that will get me attention like dating losers or abusers. My problems will get me attention. When I have attention I'll have a greater sense of control. When I have these two things, I'll feel more

worthy and lovable. Of course this is a fleeting and false sense of self-worth.

Low self-esteem deprives us of our two basic needs: to feel worthy and to be loved. If we don't feel worthy of being loved, we'll never really believe someone could actually love us. So we do anything to make sure he stays. You must love yourself in order to love someone else. If you need that person in order to keep your identity and self-worth, it is not love. It is codependence.

The woman who has a poorly defined sense of Self will define herself by the relationship. Her identity comes from the relationship. She is no longer Maggie; she is "Dillon's girlfriend." Often the person whose identity comes from the relationship will say things like, "We're going up to *our* beach house next weekend," even though it's Dillon's beach house and they've only been dating for two months. The relationship is all she talks about and she neglects her friends to spend all her time with Dillon. She stops saying "I" and only says "we." Getting your identity from the relationship is dangerous because what happens to you when the relationship ends? Do you end, too? Do you die? It feels like it to that person.

People with low self-esteem will also be less choosy when looking for a mate. A starving man will eat anything and it's no different for the person with low self-esteem. She will date anyone who looks at her. If you are desperate for a relationship, you will give in to your partner's demands and your needs will go unmet. This leads to even lower self-esteem and on and on it goes.

In the end, self-esteem boils down to two things:

1. **ATTENTION:** When you have attention from acting Constructively, you feel better about yourself. Getting

attention by acting Destructively will make you feel better in the short-term but worse in the long run.

2. **CONTROL:** Having a sense of control is one of the best determinants of healthy self-esteem. When you feel you are in control, you feel better about yourself. If you don't have a sense of control, you will feel worse about yourself.

Elderly nursing home residents that were allowed to choose what they wanted to eat from a menu, decide when to go to bed, and choose what to watch on TV lived longer, happier, and healthier lives than the elderly residents who were not given such choices. Having a sense of control is crucial to us as human beings. If we feel we have no independence and control over our lives and, to some extent, our environment, we will, for all intents and purposes, give up.

The amount of control, as well as how much and what kind of attention you're getting, determines how you cope with unpleasant and challenging experiences. How you deal with such situations will dictate how worthy you feel.

> *"Rejection is simply someone else's opinion,*
> *not everyone else's."*
>
> STEPHEN J. CANNELL

MUTINY OF THE MIND

From the moment we are born we are taught to put everyone else first. We are continuously reminded to be nice to strangers, give our guest the bigger slice of pie, complement our siblings, and above all, love thy neighbor. As a result, we spend most of our lives focused on the people around us and ignore the most important person on the planet - you. Then, we wonder why we feel frustrated, lonely, or depressed. If

134

other people ignored us as much as we ignore ourselves we might all be sucking on an exhaust pipe.

It is so important to love yourself and to express that love each and every day in order to feel worthy and loved. We all know how good it feels to be loved by another person. Imagine how great you would feel to actually be loved by you. You are the only person who can help you get exactly what you desire. No one else can provide you with the perfect relationship. There is a big difference between being self-centered and being Self centered. When you have strong, healthy self-esteem you are more centered, grounded, confident, and happy.

By ignoring or berating our Self for so long, we become disconnected and disillusioned. We then begin seeking happiness outside of ourselves. This becomes what I call a Mutiny of the Mind.

In order to create mutiny you must:

1. **Work the crew long hours with no breaks and never thank them.** How many times have you worked yourself to exhaustion and never even acknowledged yourself?

2. **Be verbally abusive.** Do you ever beat yourself up for making mistakes or for not following through on something? Have you ever berated yourself or scolded yourself for something seemingly trivial?

3. **Break the law.** For us it would be the laws of nature. We do this by not getting enough sleep, taking drugs, drinking alcohol, eating foods that are packed with preservatives, or becoming overweight or underweight.

The sad fact is most people treat their dogs better than they treat themselves. Would you give your pet drugs, cheap food loaded with chemicals and preservatives, or beat him every time he makes a tiny mistake? For most people the answer is,

"No." Yet, these same people eat poorly, become overweight, smoke cigarettes, beat themselves up over the smallest mistakes, and try to drink their problems away. This is learned very early on. If we have no other role models to help build our self-esteem, then we go through our adult relationships attempting to feel worthy rather than truly loving our partners.

You are not born with self-esteem. That's good news because it means you can improve it. Even if you didn't have healthy self-esteem as a child, you can always create stronger self-esteem as an adult. Most people are afraid to try something they feel their friends and loved ones will disagree with or ridicule. The first sign of healthy self-esteem is doing what you believe in and seeking answers about yourself even when others are against it. You are your own person.

"Believe nothing, no matter where you read it or who has said it, not even if I have said it, unless it agrees with your own reason and your own common sense."

THE BUDDHA

The person with low self-esteem gives up quickly when confronted by obstacles in the relationship. She goes through the motions but doesn't really give it all she's got. If you have high self-esteem, you persist longer when confronted by obstacles. Since you press on, you're more likely to have a successful relationship. Either way your results reinforce your beliefs, which are directly affected by the level of your self-esteem. Having healthy self-esteem causes you to feel better. But more importantly it allows you to behave in a more resourceful manner, which, in turn allows you to live better. It also allows you to *love* better.

Self-esteem boils down to two things: how we get attention and having a sense of control.

People with stronger self-esteem are more flexible and willing to admit and correct their mistakes in the relationship. Another key measure of self-esteem is the willingness to experience change. How much you feel in control when change occurs will determine the level of your self-esteem. Someone with low self-esteem is less willing to change or experience change of any kind. This is because in times of stress and change, she feels things are out of her control and she doesn't trust herself to make the right decisions. So she stays in the relationship despite the abuse. She stays in the relationship even though the love died years ago. She stays despite being unhappy. This is why she will take longer to make a decision than someone with higher self-esteem. The higher your sense of control, the higher your self-esteem. The higher the self-esteem, the higher your curiosity will be to experience new things and the less anxiety you will feel.

The higher the self-esteem, the sooner you'll dump the guy who's not right for you. Someone with healthy self-esteem says, "I don't know if I'll ever find someone who'll love me again, but you are not meeting my needs and I am unhappy. So, I'm leaving you."

The lower the self-esteem the less she feels in control. This means she'll put up with a destructive relationship longer and like herself less because of it. The person with low self-esteem will say, "I'm not sure I'll ever find anyone else who'll love me again. So I have to hold on to you, despite the fact you don't satisfy my needs and I'm unhappy because of it."

> *"I never loved another person*
> *the way I loved myself."*
> MAE WEST

SOULMATE OR CELLMATE?

Here's something you'll want to remember: In our relationships we attract someone whose self-esteem is on the same level as our own. We do not consciously think this way. In fact, what we are consciously thinking is that we have found our soul mate because we are comfortable around him and there's something so familiar about him. What's so comfortable and familiar is the way he treats you. Just like Mom and Dad treated you. Or the familiarity may come from the way he lets you treat him. Just like Mom and Dad used to treat you.

This is the worst possible match because when two people who don't think very highly of themselves get together, the relationship is a disaster. There really is no relationship. It ends up being about getting their own needs met, so they don't have anything to give to the relationship or their partner. If I have low self-esteem, I see my partner only as a source of attention and approval. When I think of you, I don't think about your wonderful traits or what makes you special. Instead, my thoughts are only about "what you can do for me" or "what have you done for me lately?"

In our relationships we attract someone whose self-esteem is on the same level as our own.

The greatest obstacle to finding true love is the fear that we don't deserve love, that we're not worthy of love. If I don't love myself, how could I possibly love someone else? If I can't give to myself, I have nothing to give to my partner. If I don't feel lovable, I won't believe you really love me. I will only end up sabotaging the relationship by becoming controlling, passive, jealous, abusive, or by cheating and lying.

Low self-esteem feeds the number one fear that if you're not good enough you won't be loved. When it comes to relationships, we tolerate more bad than we need to if we have damaged self-esteem. If something hurts our eye we get it out immediately, but if something hurts our relationship we put off doing anything about it. This stems from our two fears of not being worthy and not being loved. Let's look at some examples.

Kristen acts naïve and innocent to feel in control. By playing dumb she gets guys to give her attention and do what she wants, which makes her feel worthy. Helping a damsel in distress gives the guys the attention they seek and it makes them feel needed and more worthy. They attract each other because they both need each other to feel worthy.

Linda mothers her husband, who plays the role of the child. "Did you talk to your boss today?" she says with a babying tone. "No? Well, that's okay. You can talk to him tomorrow. You'd better practice what you want to say, though, okay? You want me to pretend I'm your boss? Okay." This allows her to take care of him, so she feels needed and therefore worthy. Linda isn't consciously aware that she's mothering him. She just thinks she's helping. Her husband is getting attention by being pampered, so he feels more worthy. Both need each other to feed their need for self-worth.

Allie manipulates with her emotions. She knows how to control her fiancée by expressing certain emotions at certain times. She also knows how he'll respond to whichever emotion she expresses. This allows her to be in control and feel more worthy. He benefits by giving in to her moods and demands so she won't leave him. Giving in to her keeps her there and that makes him feel more worthy.

Do you see how shallow their self-worth is? They feed each other's insecurities, which gives them each a sense of being in control. By feeling in control, they make themselves feel better temporarily, but in the long run their self-esteem is no healthier than before.

When Melissa yells at her husband Greg, she's doing exactly what she learned to do as a child in order to feel more worthy. If Greg were able to decipher the hidden message beneath the yelling, he'd hear Melissa's message, "I'm not good enough!" But he doesn't hear this because he's either mounting his defense or retreating and becoming more distant and resentful. When you repair and strengthen your self-esteem, the quality of your relationship grows exponentially.

If something hurts our eye we get it out immediately, but if something hurts our relationship we put off doing anything about it.

WHY DO I STAY?

Sometimes we have to admit the relationship just will not work. If you've been honest with yourself and you've cleared the Sore Spot but your relationship is still in bad shape, you have to ask yourself why you want to be in this relationship so badly.

In this case the relationship itself may be the Sore Spot. If you're getting some kind of boost to your self-worth by being in the rotten relationship, ask yourself why that is. If you're not happy, if he doesn't treat you with love and respect, if there is no communication between the two of you, then why do you remain in the relationship? How does being in that relationship make you feel more worthy?

Sometimes we don't like to admit that we've allowed our need to be loved to override our logical thinking and we stay in relationships longer than we should. We think it's better than being alone. You may be using the relationship to boost your self-worth because you feel more worthy when others see that you're in a relationship. While they may not notice how rotten the relationship really is, you cannot avoid it. In the long run, then, your self-worth will actually suffer from being in the relationship. Know when to let go and start over.

It is your choice to be a problem thinker or a solution thinker.

KIM

Kim has low self-esteem that leads her to believe she is worthy only of feeling hurt and despair, so she either chooses mates who will hurt and leave her, or she destroys the relationship by finding ways to hurt him before he hurts her. If she does find herself happy, she will immediately begin to tell herself that she doesn't deserve it. She'll think things like, "This won't last, it never does" or "There must be a big letdown right around the corner." She engages in distorted thinking patterns that are focused on negativity while ignoring the positive aspects of a situation. She is not enjoying her ride on the Mental Merry-Go-Round.

If on her way to meet her boyfriend the subway breaks down, she may ask herself, "Why does this stuff always happen to me?" If she goes to Disneyland and her favorite ride is closed, she may think, "I should have expected Space Mountain to be closed on the one day I'm here." It's often referred to as catastrophic thinking and is characterized by making mountains out of molehills. This type of thinking is a mental trap. It is very easy to slip into the cycle of problem thinking. Remember who's in charge of your thoughts. It is you who chooses to be a problem thinker or a solution thinker.

Many problem thinkers hope their partners will "fix" them and make their feelings of unworthiness and unlovable-ness go away. Our partners can provide love, support, understanding, and acceptance, but they cannot heal those

141

significant events in our past that left us with low self-esteem. Only you can change that.

> *"Failure is the condiment that*
> *gives success its flavor."*
> TRUMAN CAPOTE

THE INTROSPECTIVE DUCKLING

Remember the story of the Ugly Duckling? He did a lot of inner searching and healing to discover he was worthy of love. His family, friends, and all of society shunned him so he had to search for his inner strength all by himself. And where did he finally discover his inner beauty and self-worth? He found it in his reflection. Looking to the core of who you are is where you find the building blocks for raising your self-esteem. We develop stronger, healthier self-esteem by looking at our own reflection just as we must look to ourselves for a better relationship. Love and self-worth begins and ends inside of you.

> *"Sometimes, when I look in the mirror, I can't*
> *believe I'm in the same room with myself."*
> BERT CAMPBELL
> *SOAP*

Remember, our self-esteem - how worthy we feel we are - depends on two things:

1. The amount and the kind of *attention* we receive.

2. How much *control* we feel we have over our environment and ourselves.

When we have a sense of control and are receiving attention, we feel more worthy and more lovable. Something very

142

interesting begins to happen when you love yourself and raise your self esteem: You actually need relationships less, but the quality of the relationships you do have will be so much greater than it was before. The reason is the less we need something, the more we are able to appreciate and enjoy it. You enter into a relationship because you *want to* not because you *need* to. It's like the starving man who'll eat anything you give him. He eats anything because he needs to in order to survive. When you're not starving, you can pick and choose what and when to eat.

Use one or all of the following self-esteem exercises at least once a day. Some of these may feel awkward at first but I promise the more you use them, the more comfortable you'll feel and the more insights you'll receive. There is no right or wrong way to do this and each experience will be totally unique to you. Whatever you experience is perfect.

> ***With healthy self-esteem, you actually need relationships less, but the quality of the relationships you do have is better.***

Before we get into the other exercises, here's an easy way to feel better about yourself without writing anything down or meditating: Do something nice for someone else. Open a door for somebody; allow him to jump ahead in the grocery line if he looks to be in a hurry; smile and say hello to a stranger; compliment her choice of shirt or shoes; pay the toll for the car behind you; anonymously pay for the coffee for the gal three spots behind you in line; give a ride to the elderly woman who's waiting for the bus; let someone else take the parking space closer to the store. Use your imagination.

> *"To have more than you've got,
> become more than you are."*
>
> JIM ROHN

Doing something for others out of love or generosity instead of neediness will give your self-esteem a shot in the arm and you'll begin to feel more lovable. When you do something for others you become self-less and that makes you feel more worthy and loved. It's an interesting paradox to forget about yourself in order to feel better about your Self. When you feel grumpy and you do something nice, like help an old lady with her groceries, you feel better because you're being self-less, which raises your self-esteem and makes you feel more lovable.

WHAT HAVE I DONE FOR ME LATELY?

Our accomplishments serve to strengthen our self-esteem, as well. In order to accomplish something, we must first take a bit of a risk. For instance, if you want to date that cute guy from the coffee shop, you'll have to risk rejection and ask him out. If you want to know more about him you'll have to risk telling him more about you. No risk, no reward. When we take calculated risks and they pay off, we become more confident in our abilities and our self-esteem grows. Start small and be smart about it. The more you build upon your small accomplishments the stronger your self-esteem will become.

"You miss 100% of the shots you never take."
WAYNE GRETZKY

We need others less when we have healthy self-esteem. The less you need someone else, the more you'll enjoy being with him. It's always better to be with him because you *want* him, not because you *need* him.

The Love Meditation

Get comfortable in your favorite chair, close your eyes and take a deep breath in.

As you slowly release the breath, focus your awareness on your heart. Notice the rate at which your heart beats and listen to the "lub-dub" as it contracts and relaxes.

As you focus on the heart, think about all the things you love in this world. Think about loved ones, pets, the ocean, or anything else that fills your heart with love.

What is it about those things that cause you to love them so much? Focus all of your attention on love.

Next, begin to notice what you love about yourself. Concentrate on what is good and pure and loving inside of you. Take your time and focus on whatever it is that you love about yourself and remember to say, "I love you" every once in a while.

I Am Extraordinary!

Take 15 minutes and write in your journal or on a pad of paper all of the things that make you extraordinary. Write down everything you can think of. What are your talents, gifts, and strengths? Are you motivational, happy, an excellent coach or teacher, a good listener, a gourmet chef, a financial expert, a patient manager, a compassionate friend, ambitious, generous, friendly, or fun to be around? Make a list of all of your attributes, the things that make you so extraordinary to yourself and others. Go over this list and add any other qualities you may have omitted the first time. Don't be modest or shy. This is your moment to gloat. Go for it!

Next, make a list of all the things that make you an extraordinary partner. Are you loving, passionate, considerate, warm, caring, understanding, a good listener, or able to find the humor in difficult situations? Whatever it is write it down.

Read and re-read these lists any time you are feeling less worthy. Carry them with you at all times. You may even go one step further and ask the people around you, your loved ones, coworkers, and friends what they believe makes you so extraordinary. Offer to provide each of them with a list of their positive attributes in return. You will be amazed at how extraordinary you truly are!

I Love You

Stand in front of a mirror and make eye contact with your Self.

Gaze deeply into your eyes. Really connect with your Self. After a minute or so say, "I love you" and notice how you feel.

Next, tell your Self why you love you. For example, "I love you because you are always there for me" or "I love you because you understand me better than anyone" or "I love how ambitious you are." If you feel more comfortable saying, "I love me" instead of, "I love you" that is perfectly acceptable.

Now, close your eyes and remember a time when you felt totally confident...feel the feelings...open your eyes and look at yourself feeling totally confident; say I love you.

Close your eyes and remember a time when you were totally excited. Really feel the feelings...open your eyes and look at yourself feeling totally excited; say I love you.

You can also remember times you felt happy, loved, laughing, sexy, or any other feeling you enjoy. Recall a specific time when you felt that way. Feel the feelings again, then open your eyes and say, "I love you."

Finally, tell your Self that you will always be there for you and thank your Self.

Do this at least once a day.

I Did That!

Write down every amazing feat, every wonderful accomplishment, and every brilliant decision you can think of from the time you were born until right now. Make a list of every event, decision, or behavior that ended up making a hero out of you or just caused you to feel great. They can be as profound as saving a drowning man to something as simple as giving an elderly woman a ride so she wouldn't have to take the bus. Whatever it was that caused you or others to feel excited, amazed, energized, awe struck, pleased, happy, empowered, fulfilled, grateful, or warm inside write it down.

Pick one memory and close your eyes. Go back to that time and float right into the memory so you're looking through your own eyes. See what you saw...hear what you heard...and really feel the feelings of being in that moment once again. Stay there as long as you wish.

When you're finished, notice how you feel. Notice, also, what a truly wonderful and accomplished person you are.

Keep this list with you, add to it, and re-read it as often as you wish.

It's Okay

Close your eyes and float back to a time when you were a small child, before there ever was a Sore Spot, and see the Younger You standing in front of you. Greet Younger You with a hug and a smile. Hold Younger You in your arms and tell Younger You:

It's okay to make mistakes.
It's okay to be afraid.
It's okay to feel and express your emotions.
It's okay to express your needs.
It's okay to want attention.
It's okay to be loved.
You are safe.
You are understood.
You are loved.

Tell Younger you about all the extraordinary joys and wonderful sorrows Younger You will experience in the future. Tell Younger You about all the exciting events and people Younger You will meet and learn from. Express your love, appreciation, and gratitude for Younger You.

Now, float out to the future and notice Ideal You standing in front of you. Listen as Ideal You tells you:

It's okay to make mistakes.
It's okay to be afraid.
It's okay to feel and express your emotions.
It's okay to express your needs.
It's okay to want attention.
It's okay to be loved.
You are safe.
You are understood.
You are loved.

Listen as Ideal You tells you about all the extraordinary joys and wonderful sorrows you'll get to experience in the future. Listen as Ideal You tells you about all the exciting events and interesting people you'll meet and learn from. Listen as Ideal You expresses his/her love, appreciation, and gratitude for you.

Take a moment and integrate all that you've learned. When you're ready, come back to now and open your eyes.

14

Emotions In Motion

"Magically, when there is no enemy within there are far fewer without."

MARY-ELAINE JACOBSEN

HOUSTON WE HAVE A PROBLEM

Feeling and being are two completely different things. If you feel stupid are you stupid? No. A feeling is only a feeling. It doesn't define who you are. Some people get into trouble when they dwell on painful feelings like anger, sadness, fear, guilt, hurt, or frustration. Focusing on feelings, pleasant or unpleasant, causes them to persist. When the feelings continue, we begin to believe we are what we're feeling. If the feelings are unpleasant, we begin to believe we're an angry, frustrated, or depressed person. If I'm sad all the time, then I must be depressed. If we fall into this trap it can be difficult to get out. This is especially true if we are unaware of the thoughts that are causing all that unpleasantness.

A feeling is only a feeling.
It does not define who you are.

Negative, unpleasant, and painful feelings are useful and necessary as long as we are open to receiving the messages they contain. If we ignore their meaning we run the risk of becoming what we are feeling. We become a depressed, angry, or frustrated person. If I'm pissed off all the time, then I must be an angry person. And if I'm an angry person, then I should be pissed off all the time. It becomes a vicious cycle. But when we listen to the message within the emotion we are able to give meaning to it. This meaning allows us to cope more easily and to learn and grow from the experience. When we learn from an experience and its corresponding feelings, we do not make the same mistake again. Negative, unpleasant, and painful feelings then serve two purposes:

1. They let us know there's a problem.
2. They let us appreciate the good feelings.

Unpleasant feelings, just like physical pain, serve to let us know there's a problem. Without this signal we might never enforce our boundaries, stand up for what we believe in, or recognize a Sore Spot. We wouldn't know anything is wrong so we would keep doing what we were doing. If we didn't feel painful emotions we wouldn't seek answers or learn from our mistakes. Negative, unpleasant, or painful emotions are necessary for raising a red flag and getting our attention when there's a problem.

These same feelings also let us appreciate the good times. Without unpleasant or painful feelings, we'd have nothing with which to compare our happy or pleasant feelings. How would you know you're happy if you've never felt sad? How could you truly be grateful for the good times if you've never gone through the bad times? I can't truly appreciate winning a race if I've never lost one. We can't be grateful for the love in our life if we've never felt unloved.

"A ship in port is safe,
but that's not what ships are built for."
ADMIRAL GRACE MURRAY HOPPER

Unpleasant and painful feelings are like trusty guides that are constantly looking out for our best interests. Our best interests are feeling worthy and being loved. By feeling neglected, your emotions are telling you there's a problem. Your need to feel worthy is not being met. So the red flag goes up and you take action to do something about it. If you do something Constructive, everything will be fine. If you act Destructively, you may feel worthy for a moment but eventually you'll feel less worthy.

Remember: Thought precedes emotion. If you're feeling bad, it's because you're thoughts are sending the message, "I'm not worthy" along those millions of nerve connections. The thought alone won't move you to action because most people aren't even aware of their thoughts. In order to really get your attention, your mind knows it has to use an unpleasant or painful emotion.

Of course the danger here is that you will act Destructively, fill your need temporarily, and a Sore Spot will be created. Let's say your last boyfriend cheated on you and you were devastated. Your current partner, however, is completely trustworthy. Even though logically you know he's trustworthy, the next time he comes home late your emotional mind takes over and you feel that pit in your stomach and begin to wonder if he's lying. You could think suspicious thoughts and feel even worse. You could punish him or interrogate him. Or you could eliminate that Sore Spot, give him a hug, and welcome him home. The unpleasant feeling will subside and you will strengthen your relationship by choosing to act Constructively. When you choose how to respond rather than letting your emotions choose for you, you diminish the power of those negative feelings.

153

But how can you do this? How can you just turn your feelings on and off? You're a person, not a machine. The answer, again, can be found in the mind. Hmmm, this is a recurring theme, isn't it? Since your thoughts influence the emotions you feel, then the things you think about, past, present, and future will determine how you feel.

Remembering bad stuff makes you feel bad. Remembering good things makes you feel good. To feel good, then, all you have to do is remember or think about good things. We're constantly thinking about good and bad things anyway, we're just not consciously aware of it. By using our thoughts and memories on purpose, we can control what emotions we feel at any given time and from moment to moment.

When you choose how to respond rather than letting your emotions choose for you, the power of those negative feelings diminishes.

CHOOSING YOUR EMOTIONS

Let's take a moment and explore how we use our body every day without realizing it. For this exercise you should be standing. As you stand there, I'd like you to get sad. Think about something that makes you sad and notice as you do what happens to your posture. How are you holding your shoulders? Do you hold your head up or down? Where are your eyes looking? Notice if your rate of breathing changes and if it moves higher or lower in your chest. Do you fidget or gesture in a specific manner? What do you say to yourself when you're sad? Be aware of your facial expression and how you hold your eyebrows, nose, lips, and jaw. Is your face relaxed or is it filled with tension? Is your internal rhythm fast or slow? Be aware of your body inside and out, from head to toe, and how specifically you hold yourself when you are sad. The way you hold your body when you are sad is a habit. When you have sad thoughts your body assumes this posture. Your entire body remembers how to help you get sad and it does so by assuming this posture.

Any gesture or movement you make influences your feelings by strengthening the association between the movement and the feeling. Also, the kind of movement you make determines the direction your feelings take. Pumping your fists in the air will cause you to feel differently than clenching your fists by your side.

Our thoughts make our body assume a certain posture. This posture is so ingrained it reinforces thoughts and enhances feelings. If we assume a certain posture it will cause us to think certain thoughts because that posture has been neurologically linked to a particular pattern of thinking. When you slouch your shoulders and drop your eyes and head, it helps you to feel sad faster and more deeply. Lifting your head and standing up straight with your shoulders back will cause you to feel more energized, happy, or confident. Resting your chin on your hand may cause you to feel sad, but placing your thumb and index finger on your chin may cause you to feel smart or contemplative. The thought to strike a pose happens about five hundred milliseconds before you're consciously aware of it and helps you feel the emotion more quickly and more deeply.

Remember, the emotional mind is weighing the pros and cons of behaving a certain way. It wants to get the best emotional benefit it can from its decision. We do this when we're uncomfortable or nervous. We put our hands in our pockets or fidget to make ourselves feel more comfortable. So, it is through our posture and our gestures or movements that we are able to enhance our own thoughts and feelings.

COME ON GET HAPPY

Now, stand like you would stand if you were totally happy. How do you hold your shoulders? Is your head up or down?

Where do your eyes look? Notice what part of your chest you breathe from. Be aware of your facial expression and how you hold your mouth, eyebrows, and nostrils. What gestures do you make? What do you say to yourself when you're elated? Does that voice in your head speak quickly or slowly? Notice everything about your body inside and out from head to toe when you are totally happy. Notice the tempo of your internal rhythm. Once again, the way you hold your body when you are happy has become a habit. Your body remembers how to stand and behave in order to enhance your feeling of happiness.

From similar situations in the past your body knows where to go and how to respond. If you're accused of something, your body knows it has to get into a defensive stance. When someone's yelling at you, your body knows it needs to assume either a cowering or a fighting stance. As the mind makes a split second decision, the body follows and aids the mind in accomplishing its goal.

When I say, "get sad," you think sad thoughts causing you to feel a bit of sadness and put your body in a sad posture. This reinforces the original sad thought, causing you to feel a deeper sadness, and on and on it goes. Try to think sad thoughts while you assume the posture of being totally happy. You may find it difficult. This is true for all emotional states. Again, stand like you stand when you are sad. Get really sad. Drop your head, slouch your shoulders and move the way you move when you are really sad. As you assume this posture, I'd like you to try to think happy thoughts. Try as hard as you can. You may find this equally difficult. This is due to the nerve cells connecting mind and body. The brain thinks, "If I'm smiling, I must be happy. So, I'd better think happy thoughts." Your body and mind have been conditioned to think certain thoughts and feel a certain way when it assumes a particular posture. Try to feel sad while you skip around the block. Try to feel lethargic and tired as you march around the room.

*"Our bodies are our gardens;
our wills our gardeners."*

WILLIAM SHAKESPEARE

The purpose of changing what you're feeling at any given moment is to put yourself in a more resourceful state. When we feel bad we don't give a hundred percent. When he comes home late and you feel that pit in your stomach, you're not in a very resourceful state and you're probably not going to resolve the issue in a respectful and Constructive manner. You want to feel resourceful feelings like calmness, confidence, or compassion because you are better equipped to cope with stressful situations when you do. When someone gets violently angry how much control do they have over their behavior? Almost none. But you can be angry with your partner and still respond Constructively. We do this by utilizing more resourceful feelings like peacefulness, compassion, and so on.

FIGHT OR FLIGHT

Sometimes we think that we're just reacting. We aren't. A thought has to occur in order to do something. We have an instinct in each of us called the Fight or Flight Response. When confronted with a dangerous or stressful situation, we make a split second decision at the subconscious level to stay and fight or turn and flee. On the conscious level, we think we're just reacting. At the subconscious level, your mind makes a decision approximately five hundred milliseconds before you're aware of it consciously. The decision is based on the estimated emotional benefit for reacting a certain way. So when you step out in front of the bus, you may think your instincts pulled you back onto the curb, but your mind actually sized up the situation and made a decision of how best to respond. Once the thought occurred, the feeling of fear could be felt.

The clients I work with are always astounded when I ask them to get really sad. They're thinking, "I'm here so I *won't* feel sad. What is this clown doing?" Despite their incredulous looks, the tears begin to flow almost immediately upon my request. Of course they do, their body has been conditioned for years to feel sad when the mind decides to be sad. When I ask them to be happy they are more than able to stand tall, lift their chin, and think happy thoughts. I run them through this drill a few times and it never ceases to amaze them how quickly they're able to turn their tears on and off.

Once they experience this, they cannot dispute it. It's usually the first thing I'll do with a client so any time they say they are feeling a little low I can simply ask them to change their emotional state. Of course, if I simply told them at the start that they have the ability to change how they feel in an instant, they wouldn't believe me. However, once they have experienced it, like you just did, they are left with no excuses for feeling bad.

Just so we're clear, I'm not saying you shouldn't be in a bad mood or get pissed off once in a while. The truth is some people are inconsiderate and rude and you're going to run into them from time to time. Even a monk will express anger, frustration, sadness, and so on. It's healthy for us to express all of our emotions; that's why we have them. Just try to express them Constructively. Hey, let's face it, it feels good to be grumpy every now and then. Just be cautious of letting it consume you. If you get dumped, be sad. If he doesn't respect your boundaries, be disappointed or angry. This isn't about slapping a permanent grin on your face or pretending to be something you're not.

The point of feeling how you want when you want is twofold. First, when you're not feeling resourceful, you can simply change how you're feeling and become more resourceful. Second, nobody needs to be cast under your grumpy shadow. Be crabby all you want, but know how to conjure up a smile for coworkers and loved ones. Go off and be alone if you really feel like you can't fake it. It's okay to be cranky. It's not okay to take your mood out on anyone else or suck him or her into your negative vortex.

Sharing a bad mood or problems with a close friend is one thing. We often seek out friends to help us overcome our issues. But, if you're spreading your bad mood around to everybody, ask yourself, "What am I getting by dumping my unpleasant feelings on others? Am I doing this because it's getting me attention?"

RECALLING PAST FEELINGS

An easy way to change how you feel is to recall a specific memory when you felt the way you'd like to feel now. For instance, can you remember a time when you felt totally loved? Remember a specific time and, as you do, see what you saw, hear what you heard, and feel the feelings of being totally loved. If you are like most people you will feel the feelings you felt at that time. Recalling a past vivid experience is a simple way to feel a particular emotion. The memory or thought produces the feeling and the body complies.

To feel any feeling you want simply do the following:

Remember a time when you felt totally _____. Remember a specific time. As you go back to that time, look through your own eyes. See what you saw, hear what you heard, and feel the feelings of being totally _____.

The next time you find yourself suddenly sad, ask yourself what you were thinking just before you felt the emotion. Be aware of your posture and what your body is doing. Then recall a past pleasant experience and change what you're feeling.

15

History Repeating

*"We first make our habits,
and then our habits make us. "*

JOHN DRYDEN

Your relationships today are the result of the training or conditioning you received in your childhood. Early on we are most influenced by our parents. As we grow older, teachers, coaches, the media, heroes, celebrities, society, authority figures, siblings, and friends also have an influence on us. But the most crucial learning period for a child is from birth to around age seven. During the first seven years a child is more easily influenced than at any other time and the parents are the most influential.

*"What the child sees, the child does.
What the child does, the child is. "*

IRISH PROVERB

Children see their parents as powerful and right. They observe everything the parent does or says and seldom question their behavior. The child has to learn many things, and the parents are the teachers. Many parents think the child learns mostly when they tell them what to do or what not to do. In reality, it is when the parents don't think she is paying attention that the child learns the most. By observing our parents in every situation, from giving the silent treatment in the car to a gentle hug for no particular reason or even a hostile glance at the dinner table, the child is passively learning how to behave in relationships.

This observation and subsequent internalization of beliefs, attitudes, and behaviors is called identification. The child imitates certain characteristics and eventually internalizes them and they become a part of her. Even if the child does not admire, respect, or even like the parent, she may still identify with him or her and internalize certain attributes.

As the child grows and finds herself in similar situations she will respond how she remembers her parents responding. It must be the "right" way to respond because Mom did it that way. There are some exceptions and we'll discuss them but first, let's focus our attention on behavior. Our behavior is learned. If a behavior satisfies one or both of our basic needs we will perform that behavior again and again. Our own history continues to repeat because the behavior gets conditioned inside us.

PAVLOV'S DOGS

Conditioning is a process by which a behavior is linked with a unique stimulus. The term conditioning came out of Russian physiologist Ivan Pavlov's well-known experiments with dogs. Pavlov would ring a bell a split second before he showed the dog a steak. Upon seeing the steak the dog began to drool. The bell represents the unique stimulus that is paired with the dogs drooling behavior. The dog could have cared less about the bell. That bell, however, would soon play an important role for that dog.

Pavlov repeated this procedure many times. First, the dog heard the sound of the bell, and then it saw the steak. After a number of repetitions, the dog began to drool at the sound of the bell in anticipation of getting the steak. Initially, the response made sense for the dog. The dog heard the bell and he would get ready to eat by salivating. However, when the steak was withheld the dog continued to drool at the sound of the bell. The dog had now become conditioned to drool at the sound of the bell. It's response served no purpose but it continued to salivate, nevertheless, because it was now a conditioned response or a habit. Likewise, a lot of our responses that were learned as children no longer serve a purpose.

> *"We are what we repeatedly do.*
> *Excellence, then, is not chance; it is a habit."*
> ARISTOTLE

There are many examples of how we are conditioned to respond to various stimuli on a daily basis. Have you ever noticed how quickly, without even thinking, you jump up to answer the telephone when you hear it ring? When the traffic light turns red do you stop? Do you go when the light turns green? Do you have a favorite song that, when you hear it, sends you into a blissful frenzy? Conversely, is there a song that really makes you feel sad when you hear it? Does the smell of fresh baked bread or chocolate chip cookies make you feel a certain way? These are all examples of how a specific stimulus is able to elicit a subconscious, immediate response in each of us. Such responses have been conditioned inside of us.

MAMA AND PAPA PAVLOV

By observing what our parents said and did, we learned exactly what we had to do in order to get attention and have a greater sense of control. By being in control and getting attention, we felt more worthy and loved. Each time we got control and attention from behaving a certain way our behavior was reinforced which, after a number of repetitions, created a conditioned response. It wasn't long before we were responding without having to consciously think about it. The problem is the behavior we learned may have been Destructive. If it was it created a Sore Spot. Using the Pavlov analogy, it means:

1. **Instead of a bell we saw manipulation, abuse, control, and insecure parents.**

2. **Instead of a steak we got attention for responding in certain ways.** One day you screamed and yelled and you got attention.

3. **Instead of drooling, we became passive, controlling, sarcastic, abusive, or a loner.** We continued to do whatever we did that gave us the attention and control we needed. In other words, we became insecure and reactive to our fear of not being worthy.

Conditioned behavior is a subconscious habit. We do it without being aware of it. When you're stopped at a red light and the light turns green, you go. You don't think about going or weigh the pros and cons of proceeding, you just go. When the alarm goes off, you swat the snooze button without even thinking. It's pouting every time you don't get your way or throwing a tantrum when you're feeling ignored. When you pout or have a tantrum, you're getting attention from your partner and you're controlling the situation. Every time you receive attention and have a sense of control from behaving that way, it reinforces the behavior and strengthens that nerve cell connection. That means you'll do it again and again. Only when that behavior stops satisfying your need will you stop acting that way.

*Only when you are aware of the pattern
can you do something about it.*

WE INTERUPT THIS PATTERN...

Now, what happens when you're sitting at the light and it
turns green and, as you go, someone runs the light and slams
into the side of your car? The next time you're at a red light
and it turns green you're going to think about going, aren't
you? This is called a pattern interrupt. The car slamming into
you interrupted your "go" pattern. Now, when the light turns
green, you proceed very cautiously because you remember
the accident, which makes you consciously aware of
oncoming traffic from all sides. We want to interrupt your
Sore Spot pattern so it stops happening.

"Break one link and the whole chain falls apart."

DANISH PROVERB

Only when you are aware of the pattern can you do
something about it. Remember, awareness is nine-tenths of
the solution. The next time that Sore Spot appears, interrupt
its pattern by doing something outrageous like screaming
from the top of your lungs, "I Love Lucy!" You could
suddenly skip around the room, take your finger and diddle
your lips while you hum, cross your eyes, or pinch your
nipples. When we do something crazy like this, it jolts our
nervous system and stops that Sore Spot pattern in its tracks.
And what happens when you stop using a particular nerve
cell connection? The millions of nerve cells break away and
begin to rewire with other nerve cells. Just like the car
slamming into you, dramatically changing your thoughts and
behavior in the middle of the Sore Spot pattern will make it
difficult to run that pattern without hesitating the next time.
Let's go ahead and interrupt that pattern right now.

"A turtle travels only when it sticks its neck out."

KOREAN PROVERB

SORE SPOT PATTERN INTERRUPT

Imagine sitting in the movie theater and watching that earliest Sore Spot memory once again. I'd like you to notice the movie of your memory is now in black and white. As it plays, I want you to shout, "I LOVE LUCY!" right as the memory comes to the Destructive behavior. As you shout, I'd also like you to freeze frame it right at the Destructive behavior part and imagine whiting the rest of the film out or black it out if you wish. Float into the film and into your own body looking through your own eyes and notice the film return to color. Now, looking through your own eyes, rewind the movie in full color all the way back to the beginning as fast as you can. When the movie memory is completely rewound, float back into your seat and watch the black and white movie play forward again shouting, "I LOVE LUCY!" right at the Destructive behavior part. White or black it out, float into the film and rewind the movie in full color looking through your own eyes as fast as you can. Do this a total of five times as fast as you can or until it's very difficult to recall the memory in you mind.

We are actually scrambling the memory so it will be harder to recall. By doing this, we are getting a head start on rewiring those millions of nerve connections. Of course you should also use this interrupt whenever the Sore Spot occurs in your every day life.

If you don't want to shout, "I LOVE LUCY," feel free to do something else. Just make sure it is totally outrageous and fun.

A CHANGE OF HABIT

We are conditioned to behave a certain way in order to feel in control and to get attention from our parents. Because it works for us, we behave this way again and again and it eventually becomes a habit. We then generalize this habitual behavior to all our relationships. If yelling is how I got attention as a child, then I will yell to get attention as an adult. In my mind I'll think, "Yelling is the only thing people understand."

Habits are just conditioned behaviors that we create so we don't have to consciously think about them each time we repeat them. The perfect example is driving your car. You don't think about driving when you're in the car. But when you first learned to drive, you had to think about it. You'd drive with your hands at the "ten-o'clock and two-o'clock" positions and focus all your attention on shifting gears and watching the road while constantly checking the mirrors. You didn't play the radio or let anyone talk to you because you had to concentrate on driving. You thought, "How am I going to use the wipers, turn on the lights, steer, shift, and drive all at the same time?"

But, after a period of time and a number of repetitions, you no longer had to think about driving. It became a subconscious habit almost completely out of your awareness. Now you drive down the highway holding your cell phone in your left hand, eating a burger with your right, steering with your knee, and tuning the radio with your big toe. You have better things to do in the car than to think about driving, right? Driving has become a habit, a conditioned response that you no longer have to think about. And every time you drive, it strengthens those nerve connections.

In much the same way we learn from our parents what we have to do in order to feel in control and get attention. Once we know how to get attention and feel in control we'll continue to behave that way because it continues to make us

167

feel worthy and loved. We strengthen those nerve cell connections and make it a habit.

"Habit, if not resisted, soon becomes necessity."

ST. AUGUSTINE

WHO'S IN CONTROL?

Habits become Sore Spots when they sabotage, undermine, or destroy relationships. We think habits are out of our control but the truth is you control all your behavior, even the habits. A smoker doesn't smoke for three hours when he's at a movie because he knows he's not allowed to smoke in the theater. When you become conscious of the habit you can control and change it. Here's why: You cannot control something you're not aware of. You don't control your breathing when you're not aware of it. When you focus on your breathing it's possible to speed it up or slow it down. You're not consciously aware of walking, either. When you do become conscious of walking, you can alter your gate or mimic how someone else is walking.

Let's say that every time someone cuts you off on the highway you scream, swear, and give them the finger. This has become a conditioned response, a subconscious habit. Yet, when you're on a first date and someone cuts you off, you don't fly off the handle because you're on your best behavior and you don't want your date to think you're nuts. The truth is we can control our behavior if we just become aware of it. Most of the time we aren't aware of it and so we just react the same old way we have in the past. We think, "That's just the way I am." But it doesn't have to be. People put themselves on autopilot; they tune out and just react without thinking. Remember, you are in charge of your thoughts, feelings, and behavior.

168

You don't fix an engine unless you know there's something that needs fixing. When do you know it needs fixing? When it breaks down. You only become aware there's a problem because it's making a funny noise. Ideally, we want to become aware of the Sore Spot before we hear that funny noise, before the relationship breaks down.

***When you become conscious of the habit
you can control and change it.***

WE ARE ALL SUPER MODELS

So, the question is, how does childhood conditioning create our adult relationships? As children, we observe our parents and we either model or avoid doing what our parents do. Most of us model some behaviors while avoiding others. It's not necessarily an all or nothing decision. We may pick and choose which behaviors and attitudes to model or avoid depending on the circumstance and how it satisfies our needs. For the most part, we don't do this consciously. I may consciously imitate the way Dad walks because I want to be like him. However, reacting to conflict like Dad did is more or less a subconscious reaction from what I learned earlier in childhood. When conflict occurs, we don't have time to weigh our behavioral options, so we fall back on what we saw Mom or Dad do in similar situations.

We make subconscious notes about how our parents reacted to the way we responded to them. If our response and their reaction made us feel in control or gave us attention, we'll do it again and again. You don't have to sit down and weigh the pros and cons of responding that way. Your mind, body, and all those nerve cells know you have to continue responding that way in order to keep getting attention. For example, if you touched a hot stove burner and burned your hand, no one had to tell you not to touch a hot stove in the future. You learned all by yourself, didn't you?

TOUGH LOVE

If your father was physically abusive and would beat you for seemingly no reason – and there is NO reason for beating a child – you may have coped by becoming "stronger" and "taking it" from him. By becoming stronger, you may have noticed your father beat you less frequently. He may even have bragged about how tough you were. So you became someone who no longer felt or expressed emotions except anger, frustration, or aggression because that is how you got Dad's attention and how you felt some sense of control. You built up a tough façade around you so nobody could get to you. This made you feel more worthy and loved by your father.

On the other hand, you may have cried and became "weak" so he would notice your tears and stop beating you. When he did, you learned at a very deep level that you had to cry and be helpless in order to get attention and regain some control. Whatever your response, if it produced the results you wanted, a brand new conditioned behavior was born.

So how does it affect your relationships today? Perhaps you married or only date gentle, "weak" men because subconsciously you decided you had to be the "stronger" one. You may yearn for an intimate, loving relationship but just can't let anyone get close to you. Or perhaps you married or date men who abuse you, which serves to remind you how truly tough you are. You may subconsciously choose abusive partners because that is what is familiar and normal to you. That is how it was when you were a child. "Besides," you think, "I wasn't worthy of non-abusive love as a child and if my own father couldn't give me that, how can I expect to get it from some other guy?" When Dad hit you, he may have told you, "I'm only doing this because I love you." So you learned that men express their love by hitting women.

When parents fight the child becomes anxious and may feel the need to interrupt or stop the argument altogether. To keep the peace she may cry, throw a tantrum, and even pick a fight of her own with a sibling. She becomes a distraction in order to make her parents stop fighting. This also gives her attention and a sense of control in these situations. Once she finds a tactic that works, she will keep doing it whenever there is conflict at home. As an adult she will do whatever it takes to avoid conflict with her partner.

If your parents bought you things when you became upset, you will perceive that as love and attention. So if, as an adult, your partner doesn't buy you things, you won't feel loved. Conversely, you may resent your parents for trying to "buy" your love. Now, whenever your partner buys you something you become upset. The same goes for being listened to when you were upset or hugged when you did something well. The way you experienced love as a child is how you need to experience love as an adult. If you grew up in a chaotic environment, then you may feel uneasy when things are calm and peaceful. If you grew up in a home where everyone yelled, it will be normal for you to yell or be yelled at. If you were raised in an environment where the man controlled everything and everyone, a man you perceive to be weak because he doesn't yell or act aggressively may repulse you.

Remember, this is a subconscious process. I don't think there's a person out there who's consciously thinking she needs to be slapped or humiliated in order to feel loved. What this person is thinking consciously is, "Why am I so bad? I deserve to be hit because I'm a bad person. I've got to be a better person. Then he'll stop hitting me and really love me." This distorted thinking pattern began in childhood and continues to perpetuate Sore Spots in adult relationships. We'll delve further into this a bit later. First, let's look at how this distorted thinking pattern was created and how it turned into a conditioned response.

There are three ways we learn from interacting with our parents. Almost everything we learn comes down to:

1. What we **see**

2. What we **hear**

3. What we **experience**

What we see, hear, and experience as children helps shape the way we'll behave in our romantic relationships. We may deliberately pay attention to specific behaviors in situations like resolving a conflict or playfully making dinner together. We do this by observing and making mental notes or asking questions regarding those responses. Other times we may passively notice our parents' behaviors without giving them much conscious thought at all. While the behaviors and responses may seem like background noise at the conscious level, at the subconscious level they are being organized, labeled, and filed away. Either way, your parents are modeling how to behave in relationships and you're taking it all in.

"Habits are cobwebs at first; cables at last."
CHINESE PROVERB

I HEARD THAT!

What we're raised with is familiar to us and so we subconsciously seek out what's familiar. Of course we do learn constructive habits from our parents, but it's the Sore Spots that are causing pain in our relationships. So how do we create the habits that develop into Sore Spots? We establish a belief first. The belief that if I act like *this* then I'll get *that* response; if I cry I will get attention. When you hear or tell yourself something enough times, you start to believe it. As a child, this is especially true.

One of the ways we create a belief is through verbal conditioning or what we heard as a child. Growing up, did you hear things like these?

- Just ignore her…she'll stop crying.
- Don't make waves.
- You shouldn't have sex before you're married.
- Yelling is the only thing you understand.
- You can't do anything right.
- You're worthless.
- You were a mistake. We didn't want you.
- Children should be seen and not heard.
- Boys are more aggressive than girls.
- Women are gold diggers.
- Women are emotionally insecure.
- Women are needy and dependent.
- Women are high maintenance.
- Women can't succeed in a man's world.
- The woman should serve the man.
- Men are cheating bastards.
- Men aren't very affectionate.
- Men are insensitive.
- Men can't commit.
- Men are selfish.
- Men are controlling.
- All men want is sex.
- I need a husband to support me.
- Some day my Prince will come.
- Happily ever after.

How are we supposed to live happily ever after if we hear all that other garbage? The unfortunate truth is that if you heard statements like these growing up, they're still with you in your subconscious mind and are running your relationships. They have become that inner parental voice that holds you back, criticizes you, or makes you feel guilty.

NADINE

An example of the power of verbal conditioning came at the expense of one of my clients. Nadine never enjoyed sex with her boyfriend. If she did allow herself to enjoy sex she felt guilty afterward. Obviously, this was a problem for her and her boyfriend. He was beginning to think he was doing something wrong.

As we worked, she shared that when she was growing up her Mom used to tell her, "Sex is disgusting. You should only have sex to get pregnant; otherwise you're just a slut, and sluts are worthless."

Nadine was verbally conditioned to believe that sex is bad. Therefore, her mind linked "sex" with being "dirty" and "bad." At the subconscious level, she doesn't want to be 'bad.' Therefore, she can't have sex or, if she does, she shouldn't enjoy it. She doesn't want her mother to disapprove of her and, based on her beliefs, if she had sex, Mom wouldn't approve. Therefore the only thing to do is not have sex or if she does, to not enjoy sex.

Now you would think that in choosing between good sex and gaining Mom's approval, most people would take the sex. Not a chance. Logically it may make sense. But remember, in a showdown between logic and emotion, emotion almost always wins.

Understanding logically that it is wrong for your father to beat you doesn't mean your emotional mind agrees.

Emotionally, the need for attention may be so great it will overtake logical thought and accept the abuse as love. Any attention is better than none. Recall the jar of rice water that turned black because it was ignored.

MONKEY SEE, MONKEY DO

What is unspoken is implied through actions rather than words. The way your father treated your mother or how your mother treated you, are examples. What we saw growing up is the second way we are conditioned. What did you see as a child? What was your parents' relationship like when you were growing up?

- Were they more like bosses or parents?

- Did they express love or withhold it?

- Were they lovers or fighters?

- Were they competitors or companions?

- Did they express love easily or was it a struggle?

- Were relationships a source of joy or the cause of bitter disappointment at home?

- Did they want obedience or cooperation?

- Were they flexible or rigid?

- Did they inspire or intimidate?

Relationships are made up of trust, compassion, support, honesty, and respect. How many of these did you see growing up? If you're like me, the answer is not many. If we didn't see it, we most likely didn't learn it. The old saying, "Monkey see, monkey do" applies here. We are just little monkeys watching and learning and doing what our parental monkeys do. As kids, we don't know any better. We learn just about everything by modeling because we have no one with whom to compare our parents. So we take their behaviors as the right way to give and receive control and attention. And, we know that when we get attention and have a sense of control, we feel more worthy and loved.

A friend of mine shakes her leg constantly whenever she's sitting down. She can't control it because, she says, "My Mom did it, my grandma did it…it's like a genetic habit." It may seem like it's genetic, but that's only because the pattern has been learned through generations and has never been broken. It's become a subconscious behavior, a habit.

It is similar to the story about a woman who prepares a ham for dinner by cutting off both ends before putting it in the pan. Her confused husband asked why she cuts off the ends. "That's how my Mom cooked it," she replied. So they asked Mom why she cut off the ends of the ham. Mom replied, "That's how my Mom cooked it." So they decided to call grandma and ask why she cut off the ends of the ham. Her answer? "Because my pan was too small."

"The apple doesn't fall far from the tree."
PROVERB

Most of the time we don't ask why they do the things they do; we just follow our parents' lead. Monkey see, monkey do. We think, "They're my parents so they must know the best way to do things." The same thing occurs when buying your favorite brand at the store. We reach for the same brand our mother used and her mother used before that. We don't even think about it. We don't even notice the other cheaper, just as effective brands right next to our brand. Why? Habit. Subconscious behavior. We rationalize our behavior by saying, "I just like my brand." Maybe. But how can you compare it if you've never tried anything else? The same is true of Constructive responses versus Destructive Sore Spot responses. We are truly creatures of habit and those habits are formed very early in our lives. So it is crucial that we become aware of them.

THE HEAT OF THE MOMENT

The third way we are conditioned is through our experiences. What we experience and how we respond to those experiences helps create a Sore Spot. What did you experience when you were young regarding relationships and love? Were you rejected, neglected, abused, respected, showered with unconditional love, or were conditions put on the love you received? These experiences are extremely important because they shape the beliefs you now live by.

A girl who never gets attention starts yelling and screaming. Her parents pay attention to her, whether its yelling back at her or calming her down or giving her what she wants, it's attention and she's getting it. Now she knows how to get attention so she keeps doing it whenever she feels neglected or ignored. As an adult, this behavior is so ingrained it's become a subconscious habit. She no longer sees that it comes from her. Instead she sees it as something "he" does that sets her off. We're so used to responding or behaving a certain way that we don't see ourselves as part of the problem or cause. The last thing we want to do is look at ourselves as the problem. We already feel flawed from childhood and we don't want to be reminded of that anymore.

We rarely look at it this way. We think there's always something wrong with the people we date. We don't stop to think that what was seen, heard, and experienced as children has been applied to every one of our adult relationships. If what was seen, heard, and experienced was healthy, loving, and appropriate, we stand a better chance of experiencing healthy relationships. If most of it was abusive, controlling, and painful, we're more prone to experience Sore Spots in our relationships.

We're so used to responding or behaving a certain way that we don't see ourselves as part of the problem or cause.

YOU GO YOUR WAY, I'LL GO MINE

Since human beings were given the gift of free will, the ability to choose for themselves, you'll find two children that respond differently to the same parents. They choose to model different behaviors. Identical twins observe the same relationship between Mom and Dad. Now, the relationship gets pretty bad. There's lots of yelling and screaming and name-calling. One twin sees Mom dominating Dad. She thinks, "Mom is overbearing and manipulative and Dad is helpless. I feel sorry for Dad." So she sides with and models Dad in this situation. When she does this, she subconsciously chooses to be weak and play the victim in relationships. The other twin sees the same behavior but she notices how strong Mom is compared to Dad. She subconsciously chooses to be the strong one in relationships and she models her mother's behavior. Even identical twins make their own separate choices.

MONICA

Monica grew up watching her mother demean and humiliate her father in front of everyone from friends and family to co-workers and complete strangers. Over the years Monica saw her father slowly become only a shell of the man he used to be. She grew to hate her mother for treating her father so cruelly. As a result, Monica sided with her father. Her mother used to tell Monica, "You have to be tougher and stronger than men to be successful in this world."

She hated that her mother played the tough bitch by demeaning her father. Yet, even though she hated her, Monica finds herself following the very example her mother set growing up. Monica can't let anyone get close to her and runs away the minute things start to get serious in her relationships. If she gets too close it's a sign of weakness. So in order to be tough and remain stronger than her man she keeps him at a distance. She is acting like her mother and hates herself because of it. You don't have to like a parent to model them.

"The good things which belong to prosperity are to be wished, but the good things that belong to adversity are to be admired."

SENECA

ANITA

Sometimes we develop beliefs from observing our parents without modeling them. Anita's parents never showed affection for one another. She cannot remember even one time her father said, "I love you" to either her or her mother. As a child, Anita stood by and watched her parents argue on a seemingly daily basis. The only time they didn't argue was when they weren't speaking to each other. After graduating high school, Anita moved away to college. While she was in school, she learned her father had been cheating for years and her mother was finally seeking a divorce. Anita was twenty-two years old and had never seen what a loving, respectful, and happy relationship was like.

When she turned thirty-five, Anita realized she was still single and began to look for reasons why. While she could get a boyfriend whenever she wanted, she realized she would always end the relationship when it began to get serious. Anita had a fear of commitment. "I don't want to end up like my parents," she said. "I've never seen a good relationship so I'm very skeptical to think love can last."

Sadly, this is an increasingly common theme. Many people are afraid to get married because they don't want to turn out like their parents. At the same time they don't know how to create a better relationship because they were never taught these skills growing up. As a result, they long for the very thing they fear: commitment. Anita was conditioned to believe all relationships end up like her parents. While she yearns to be close to someone, she won't allow herself to get too close. So she finds relationships that will create enough distance that she won't have to fully commit. Choosing inappropriate or married partners, cheating, arguing, or working too much are all ways of creating distance within a relationship.

Conditioning is the reason we date someone who treats us like our parents did or makes you treat him like your parents treated you. In this way, our partner feels normal and familiar to us. Of course, some people only know conflict, fear, abuse, and walking on eggshells from their childhood. While they know it's not Constructive, it is what they know, and so it's familiar and normal. These people know the difference between Constructive and Destructive behaviors. They are free as adults to make their own decisions. So why don't they? They're no longer aware that the behavior stems from childhood. This is why almost everyone blames his or her partner. They don't even think to look at themselves as the cause.

As children we can't even imagine that Dad or Mom are wrong. Instead, we think we deserve the abuse, criticism, or jokes at our expense because we're so bad. In the process, our self-esteem takes a hit and our lack of confidence affects every relationship we have from that point on.

YOUR INNER CHILD CHOOSES YOUR LOVERS

Children constantly watch and listen to their parents. They have nothing to compare their parents to, so they take their behavior as normal; everybody acts like this. Every man yells at his wife until she cries. Every mother calls her child names and makes a scene in front of the whole store. Your inner child chooses your partners by looking for someone who will treat you in that familiar way or someone who lets you treat him the way your parents treated you.

We separate from our parents' values, beliefs, and authority during adolescence and turn to other adult role models like coaches, teachers, athletes, and celebrities. When we're older, we may question some of what we learned from our parents. But the early training is still there, lurking.

When I dated my high school girlfriend, I remember seeing how her parents behaved so lovingly toward each other. I thought, "That's different. I want that." But even though I wanted it, I didn't know how to get it because it was so foreign and unfamiliar to me. I started to imitate them and began treating my girlfriend like her Dad treated her Mom. But at the first sign of conflict, I didn't know how to handle it, so I fell back on what was familiar and started yelling and storming around. I had to unlearn those old behaviors and relearn new ones.

If you've ever watched kids on their first day of school you will see children staying close to their parent. Mom is safety. In case anything happens, the child knows Mom is right there; she's safe and familiar in the face of these threatening and unfamiliar surroundings. As adults, when we get into uncomfortable or unfamiliar situations in our relationships, we fall back on our familiar safety net - our parents - and how they responded in similar situations.

Sometimes children are witness to the worst parents in the world and don't even know what the "opposite" of them would be. Instead of giving up, they turn to other role models outside the family like the families they see portrayed on TV or the Jones' who live next door. The child knows what's "bad" and so she seeks a model for what's "good." It could be a friend's parents, celebrities, a favorite teacher, coach, or an older friend or sibling.

> *"Bad habits are like a comfortable bed;*
> *easy to get into but hard to get out of."*

PROVERB

ANDREA

At age ten, Andrea had to raise her younger siblings. The daughter of alcoholic parents, she was forced to raise her brother and sister yet received no praise for it. As a result, she never experienced a childhood. She was conditioned to take care of everyone else and disregard her own needs. All she knows is taking care of others.

As a child, Andrea desperately wanted her parents' attention. Instead, she had to stand by, feeling invisible, while her younger brother and sister received all the love and attention. As a child, she was there to take care of others. Otherwise she didn't matter. She became a mini-adult. Her needs were ignored so she had to deal with loneliness while denying her own needs. Since she had little control, except over her siblings, she became controlling of others. Subconsciously knowing that any kind of attention is better than no attention, Andrea learned to get a sense of control and attention by parenting, controlling others, and making adult decisions. This made her feel more worthy and loved.

As an adult, Andrea rebelled against her parents by not drinking. She even married a non-drinker. But she kept running her childhood pattern of how to get attention by marrying an infantile, insecure, verbally abusive, frustrated man. By doing this, subconsciously, she was able to keep running her pattern for getting and recognizing attention the only way she knew how as a child: by chasing after love. She chased after her parents' love and never caught it. This same pattern repeated itself when she married a man who was incapable of loving her or their children.

It is not a conscious behavior. Andrea is simply doing what she was conditioned to do as a child. She is unhappy because she doesn't have what she wants and doesn't know how to ask for what she wants because she cannot define what she wants. How can you ask for what you want when you don't even know how to describe it? Deep inside, what she really wants is to feel worthy and loved. Only by clearing away the Sore Spots will she be able to enjoy the relationship for which she yearns.

PETRINA

Petrina still feels guilt over her father leaving when she was a child. As a child, she thought that if she just loved him more, he would come back. He never did. Now Petrina fears the men in her life will abandon her so she clings to them and tries to prove her worth so they won't leave her. She loves them more and more but they all eventually leave her.

Petrina attracts men who take from her but never give anything back. They are controlling and resent her for being too needy. But being needy is what's familiar for Petrina, and if it's familiar it represents normalcy and comfort. She knows what she can expect from it. The rules haven't changed, but she tries to change them and get it right the next time, to no avail.

ALYSSA

Alyssa's mother was abusive and unpredictable. She would throw tantrums unexpectedly and seemingly over minor events. Alyssa's mother was nice to her older brother and younger sister but incredibly mean to her. Looking back,

Alyssa realized her mother was jealous of her fathers' pretty secretaries.

Her mother had just gone through a hysterectomy that probably made her feel less worthy. At the same time, Alyssa was going through some changes of her own as she began menstruating and developing breasts. Alyssa came to realize her mother was jealous and felt threatened by *her*. Her mother was feeling less worthy and less of a woman after the hysterectomy while Alyssa was becoming a woman. So, in order to feel superior, her mother lashed out, cut Alyssa down to size, and made her feel less worthy.

How did this affect Alyssa's relationships as an adult? She felt worthless and, therefore, became the giver in the relationship, never asking or expecting anything in return. She gave up control and allowed herself to be controlled. She dated controlling and abusive men. These men belittled her and showed her little, if any, respect. She would use sex to get or keep a man. In the end she always felt frustrated and lonely.

Before I worked with her she blamed all the men she dated. There was something wrong with all of *them*. When I guided her through this program, she was able to notice some things she was doing that she learned as a child from what she saw, heard, and experienced in her interactions with her mother. Alyssa completed this program and has taken charge of the quality of her relationships. She is better able to screen her dates for what she really wants in a man instead of what her inner child was choosing for her. She's also now in charge of how she responds in situations where her Sore Spot used to respond for her.

In order to do this she had to be honest with herself about her past and let go of the denial and rationalizations such as:

- Mom only yelled at me because she was stressed out from work.

- I deserved to be yelled at because I was a bad daughter.

- Dad didn't stop Mom or help me because he was busy with other things. Besides, he never really knew how Mom treated me.

Not only did she have to sort through her relationship with her mother, she also had to deal with her father's lack of intervention and denial. As long as you rationalize, you cannot get to the truth. If you don't admit the truth, you can't heal your Sore Spot. Divorced people who remarry almost always pick someone who's like the person they just divorced. Until you become aware of the Sore Spot and commit to healing that pattern, you will continue to make the same mistake again and again.

We learn a great deal from our parents. From the time we are born, we observe how our parents interact with each other and with us. If we grow up in a single parent household we witness how our parent interacts romantically with others of the opposite sex. By the time we are seven years old the foundation for our personality is set. This means that our parents play the largest and earliest role in the development of our personality. What we see, hear, and experience from observing our parents makes us choose to model or avoid doing what our parents do.

We make a subconscious decision, based on the information we have at the time, to follow our parents' lead or go in the opposite direction. This modeling then helped shape the beliefs and values you have today. It also determined the quality of your relationships because those beliefs and habits get generalized to every relationship in adulthood. The good news is all behavior is learned, even the Sore Spots. The better news is if it is learned, it can be unlearned.

One of the main reasons we attract or become our parents in our relationships is to finally resolve our childhood hurts. We subconsciously replay childhood conflicts in our adult relationships in hopes of getting it right this time. Most often we do not. The same scenarios play out and we continue to get the same results. The reason is most people aren't aware of how they're contributing to the problem so they continue responding the way they've always responded. As a result, we feel a greater sense of loss when the relationship ends because our hopes of "fixing" our past end with it. You must understand the Mental Merry-Go-Round and take charge of what you think, feel, and do if you are to heal your Sore Spot.

All behavior is learned and that means it can be unlearned.

Ask yourself three questions:

1. Is my partner treating me the way my parents treated me?
2. Am I treating my partner the way my parents treated me?
3. Are my thoughts treating me the way my parents treated me?

If the answers to any of these are "yes" and it's causing you to feel bad, it's a Sore a Spot and you need to get rid of it.

Become aware of your thoughts and where they come from. Notice the thoughts that got their roots from your parents. For instance, when you catch yourself thinking, "I'm stupid," you might say to yourself, "Hey, that was pretty abusive. Sounds like Dad." If you find yourself thinking, "He wouldn't want to marry me," you could think, "Hmmm…there's Mom's limiting belief rearing its ugly head." Forget about denying a thought. Just be aware of it and then let it go. Ask yourself, "Does this thought accurately reflect who I am or is it just childhood conditioning? Is it my fear of not being good enough or is it my parents' limiting belief?"

> *"Problems cannot be solved at the same level*
> *of awareness that created them."*
>
> ALBERT EINSTEIN

If you have the luxury of discovering what your parents' childhood was like, you are better able to see how they were just doing what they were taught. It may not have been the best or right way, but it was all they knew. You now know better and you can break the cycle.

16

I'd Like to Thank My Mom and Dad

"If you bungle raising your children, I don't think whatever else you do well matters very much."

JACQULINE KENNEDY ONASSIS

We know we learn a lot of our adult patterns from what we saw, heard, and experienced as a child. But what specifically were our parents like? How did they give us love and attention and what did we learn to do to get their love and attention? The amount and type of love and attention our parents gave us determined what kind of partner we are in our adult relationships. We figured out how to get love and attention based on how our parents behaved and how we responded to them.

Let's take a look at what your parents might have said or done and how it may have impacted your adult relationships. We know that children imitate those they consider to be warm, supportive, or powerful. We also know a child needs a consistent and ongoing connection with a mother or father. If this connection is inconsistent, disrupted, or nonexistent, the child's self-worth will suffer.

We observe and interact with our parents to learn how to express love and how we need others to behave so we know we're loved. This give-and-take of love and attention with our parents determines how we feel about others and ourselves. We then apply what we learned to all our relationships. This is the basis of our intimate relationships as adults and the beginning of our Sore Spots.

When we received attention and had a sense of control, we felt more worthy and loved. How much and how often they expressed their love and gave you attention will determine what you feel is the normal way to show love and attention. You also learn exactly what you have to do to get their love and attention.

> *"If you cannot get rid of the family skeleton,*
> *you may as well dance with it."*
> GEORGE BERNARD SHAW

According to child psychoanalyst John Bowlby, there are three general categories of love and attention we experienced as children that subsequently cause us to relate to our adult partners in Constructive or Destructive ways. They are:

1. **Consistent** love and attention
2. **Inconsistent** love and attention
3. **Nonexistent** love and attention

CONSISTENT

Consistent love and attention from the parents allows the child to feel worthy of being loved. This child doesn't get anxious about intimacy as an adult. She knows she is worthy of being loved and is comfortable in her skin. She gives love and attention to her partner freely because she knows and trusts it will be reciprocated. She feels confident to be herself and that she'll still be loved.

INCONSISTENT

When the parents are inconsistent in responding to their child's needs, the child tries to cope with the parents' rejection. These children desperately try to get their parents' attention by crying or yelling loudly and long enough that the parents feel guilty and respond. Do you know anyone who still does this?

As an adult, she clings to her partner or punishes him if he doesn't respond to her needs. She is either anxious or ambivalent about expressing or receiving love. She continuously worries if her partner really loves her or not and, as a result, does not trust her partner. In fact, she often displays jealous behavior toward her partner while simultaneously smothering him in the relationship.

NONEXISTENT

When the parents emotionally or physically reject the child's needs, the child learns to ignore her needs and emotions because she knows her parents will reject them anyhow. She had her attempts at getting love and attention stymied by her parents so she adopts the attitude of "every woman for herself."

Feeling and expressing emotions is as much a human need as eating and sleeping are.

The parent says something like, "Stop crying or I'll give you something to cry about" and the child learns she shouldn't cry because what she's feeling is not valid. It's like saying, "Stop being hungry. There's nothing to be hungry about." When a parent says, "Don't you say no to me" it only invalidates the child's opinion and squashes her independence. Saying, "Who do you think you are?" invalidates the child's existence, independence, opinion, and self-worth. Feeling and expressing emotions is as much a human need as eating and sleeping are. I was in the grocery store and overheard a mother tell her crying child, "If you don't shut up, I'm going to leave you here." You don't have to be abandoned as a child to have a fear of abandonment as an adult. The very threat of abandonment works just as well.

When these children become adults they find it difficult to be close to anyone. They believe they cannot depend on others and constantly struggle with trusting their partners. This lack of trust acts like a wall that keeps intimacy at a safe distance. Another wall that is common for them as adults is infidelity. These children will be emotionally unavailable to their partner, will suppress their emotions, and will most likely avoid any attachment at all.

Now, these are very general patterns and as human beings we don't all fit neatly into one of these packages. It's more likely you are somewhere between these extremes or a combination of them.

When parents are inconsistent with their love and attention toward a child, or if that love and attention is nonexistent, the child's self-esteem is affected. The result for you as an adult is feeling you're not worthy and not loved. The following subconscious thought pattern emerges: If you commit, he may discover the real you and you think, since you're not worthy, he won't like what he sees so he'll leave you. That means you'll be unloved. You may also think, "If my own parents wouldn't love me, how can I expect anyone else to love me?" And of course when he does leave you say, "I knew it!" More importantly, it reinforces your thought, "If he discovers the real, unworthy me, he won't love me," which reinforces those nerve connections and you have a very unpleasant ride on the Mental Merry-Go-Round.

PARENTS BEHAVING BADLY

Healthy parenting includes putting up boundaries and guidelines for the child. Boundaries act like fences around a farm. They allow the horses to roam anywhere they wish inside the fenced area. The fence keeps them from wandering into the wrong areas.

> *"In the final analysis it is not what you do for your children but what you have taught them to do for themselves that will make them successful human beings."*
>
> ANN LANDERS

Unhealthy parenting is like burying land mines. Rather than putting up a fence and letting the child wander within the parameters of that fence, some parent's plant land mines and wait for the child to step on one. When she does, they explode and the child is left wondering what happened. This is confusing for the child because she doesn't know what she can or cannot do. Sometimes she can do something and other times she's punished for doing it. This leaves her second-guessing herself and feeling anxious and unworthy in relationships.

> *"Children are the sum of what parents contribute to their lives."*
>
> RICHARD L. STRAUSS

PARENTING STYLES

Let's look at seven general parenting "styles" that lead to Sore Spots in our adult relationships.

1. **PLEASE ME:** Please Me parents put conditions on their love. They give the child love and attention only when the child has "earned" it. If the child doesn't please, she doesn't get love and attention. The child hears the message, "I love you, but only if you do what I say." So the child learns that love is dependent upon being good and doing what others want rather than what she herself wants. As an adult, she'll both ignore her own goals and aspirations and cater to those of her partner or she'll put her own needs ahead of his.

2. **SELF-CENTERED:** These parents are overbearing and view their own desires as being the same as their children's. They say things like, "I want you to be a doctor. So you'll be a doctor because I know that's what you want, too," and "I am always there for you so you'd better always be there for me." If a child doesn't go along with the parent's wishes, the parent feels rejected and punishes the child. As an adult, she may smother her partner or keep her distance emotionally.

3. **JEKYLL AND HYDE:** Jekyll and Hyde parents are extremely volatile. Wild mood swings are an every day occurrence as well as unpredictable and inconsistent discipline. For these parents it's all or nothing: love or hate, affection or abuse. They often try to offset one emotional outburst with the exact opposite. They may beat her with a hairbrush one moment and lovingly stroke her hair with it the next. As a result, the child is constantly walking on eggshells, trying to avoid doing anything wrong because she doesn't want to cause any problems. She starts to believe she is a bad person and deserves to be mistreated. In this way she accepts blame for *their* behavior and believes she can do something to

change it. Sadly, she cannot. As an adult, she may let her partner mistreat her just like Mom and Dad did.

4. **OBSESSIVE:** Obsessive parents push their children to be perfect in every way because they need to live out their failed dreams through the child. If the child fails to live up to expectations, the punishment may come in the form of physical or verbal abuse. These parents rarely, if ever, offer praise. Some kids may even refuse to outdo their parents thinking, "If I'm better than my parents, they won't love me anymore." Every time the child reaches for the bar, the parents raise it higher, just out of reach. Now, every time her partner makes a comment, she takes it personally and overreacts.

5. **DICTATORS:** Dictator parents are extremely rigid in their behaviors and attitudes. They have to know everything about their children at all times. Rules are strictly enforced. They expect the child to be compliant or suffer the consequences if they're not. As an adult, she may be very strict and demanding or extremely private and withdrawn from her partner. Or she might rebel completely and break rules and push the limits whenever she can. She may set out to prove that no one can ever control her again.

6. **TORMENTORS:** These parents emotionally, verbally, physically, or sexually abuse their children. They constantly demean their children in order to feel superior to them. Physically abusive parents can't control themselves and often blame the child, saying what she did caused them to hit her. This makes the child believe she deserves to be mistreated and her self-esteem suffers as a result. Usually, abuse is the only attention the child gets from the parent. And, like the jar of rice water that turned black when it was ignored, any attention is better than no attention. Verbal abuse is just as insidious and may come directly or indirectly. Direct verbal abuse is name-calling like

"moron," "you're no good," "dumb ass," "you must be someone else's child," "ugly," "worthless," or "unwanted." Indirect verbal abuse comes in the form of sarcasm, jokes at their expense, and degrading nicknames. When the child feels hurt, the parent says, "What's the matter; can't you take a joke?" or "You've got to be tough in this world," or "You have no sense of humor." A child cannot distinguish between a joke and reality. As a result, she believes what is said about her. The child thinks, "If you say I'm stupid, then I must be. If you say I'm ugly and worthless, then I am." Children believe what their parents tell them. When a child is abused, whether physically, verbally, emotionally, or sexually, anger and rage are repressed because they cannot express it. This repressed hostility can cause emotional as well as physical illness. As an adult, she abuses her partner or allows her partner to abuse her.

7. **DEPENDENT:** Lacking parenting skills, the Dependent parent controls the child using guilt or demanding to be taken care of. These parents often vent their emotional issues or sexual problems onto the child. Instead of parenting, they try to "buddy up" with the child. As a result, she attends to her parents' needs and disregards her own. In her adult relationships she'll pick selfish partners in order to repeat her pattern of disregarding her needs so she can tend to those of her partner. Tending to the needs of other's is how she received attention as a child and she continues that behavior as an adult.

"Children need love,
especially when they don't deserve it."
HAROLD HULBERT

Remember, human beings are complex creatures. As such, you may see your parents in one or more of these 'styles.' A parent doesn't have to swing to the extremes listed above. If the parent displays a milder form of any style, the child will still make subconscious decisions based on her own perceptions. Once the choice is made, the child will begin to act in accordance with her decision.

JERRI

Jerri's father had unpredictable mood swings and tantrums. As a child, she was anxious when her father was around because she never knew when he'd blow up or what she did to deserve it. Because Jerri never knew what she did to cause her fathers' tantrums and abuse, she grew up second-guessing and blaming herself. The abuse left Jerri feeling stupid and worthless. Her feelings didn't matter. She felt invisible and always tried to do things perfectly so others would notice her. As an adult, Jerri was shy and intimidated around authority figures. It was only after going through this program that she was able to raise her self-esteem to a healthy level and interact with everyone, authority figures or not, on the same level without anxiety.

MAYA

Maya's parents continually told her she would never amount to anything. Now, at age 39, she feels her life has been meaningless because she has never done anything she truly loved. Moreover, Maya can't seem to find anything she's passionate about. As a result, she goes through life like a zombie.

As a child, Maya had a couple options. She might have decided to prove her parents wrong and constantly overachieves to be better than everyone. In this case, Maya chose to prove her parents right and hasn't achieved anything she is proud of. As children, we view our parents as right and powerful, so we accept what they tell us and we don't want to hurt them by proving them wrong. This is the decision Maya made at the subconscious level. Until she decides otherwise, she will continue to be a passionless, obedient daughter.

No person fits neatly into one little package. We all have our unique experiences and responses to those experiences. Understanding your parents' style will help you become more aware of how it contributed to the Sore Spot in your relationship.

> *"Children are likely to live up to*
> *what you believe in them."*
> LADY BIRD JOHNSON

From observing and interacting with our parents we learn:

1. How to express love.
2. What we have to do to get love and attention.
3. What others need to do so we know we're loved.

This give-and-take of love and attention with our parents determines how we feel about others and ourselves. We then apply what we've learned to all of our relationships. This is the basis of our intimate relationships as adults, and the beginning of a Sore Spot as well. How we respond and the development of our self-esteem depends upon whether our parents' love and attention is consistent, inconsistent, or nonexistent.

OTHER ADULT INFLUENCES

Our parents are our earliest and most important role models. But we can't rely solely on them our entire lives. After approximately seven years of age we begin to look away from our parents for clues on how to behave in relationships. We begin to look to teachers, coaches, the parents of friends and neighbors, older siblings, celebrities, and television family role models.

MIA

Mia has a sister that is seven years older. She watched as her sister married a nice man who never rocked the boat. At first it seemed like a match made in heaven. After a year of marriage, though, Mia's older sister found herself overwhelmed with a child, exhausted from constant parenting, and bored with her husband.

Consequently, Mia was on the receiving end of many conversations with her sister about how the sex was no longer exciting and how she felt the only thing her husband was good for was putting food on the table. Between the ages of fourteen and eighteen, Mia had a front row seat to how bad a relationship can be when one or both partners have given up.

From observing her sister's relationship for four years, Mia decided she never wanted a relationship like that. Unfortunately, in making this decision she subconsciously began pushing her boyfriends away when she felt they were getting too close. Although she consciously yearns for a soul mate, she subconsciously sabotages any chance for happiness because she sees all relationships ending up like her sister's marriage.

Sometimes a relationship somewhere along the line left us feeling wounded in some way. For instance, a long-time boyfriend may have cheated on you. The incident may have left you unable to trust men. Or perhaps it's kept you from getting too close emotionally ever since. Because he cheated, you became bitter and held back more emotionally in your next relationship. When that relationship didn't work out, you became more emotionally distant in the next relationship. With each subsequent relationship, your bitterness increased and you became more distant. Now you find yourself incapable of getting close to anyone. If you can trace your Sore Spot to a former partner, simply reference that boyfriend and that relationship when answering the questions at the end of this chapter.

If you're wondering where your Sore Spot came from, start with what you learned from your parents. If it has nothing to do with your parents, then think back to which adult authority figures made the biggest impression upon you. Then, as you go through the questions at the end of this chapter, simply replace the word 'parents' with the uncle, sister, neighbor, teacher, friend, or coach who influenced you the most.

"What's done to children, they will do to society."

KARL MENNINGER

Were your parents tyrants? Did they try to be your best friends rather than parents? Was there physical or verbal abuse?

- **If** you always had to chase your father's love, perhaps you replay the issue by chasing men who won't commit to you.

- **If** your parents were neglectful, perhaps you learned that you weren't worthy of love and attention from anyone else.

- **If** your parents gave you love and attention when you first took a few steps but the next time said, "You can do better than that," maybe you believe you always have to "go the extra mile" in your relationships.

- **If** you pick all the wrong guys, you may be doing it because you don't think the "right" guys will find you worthy; much like your father didn't.

These are all examples of how early childhood events create issues in our adult relationships.

"Good timber does not grow with ease; the stronger the wind, the stronger the trees."

J. WILLARD MARRIOTT

QUESTION 1

How were you conditioned? What did you <u>see</u>, <u>hear</u>, and <u>experience</u> from your parents that laid the foundation for the Sore Spot in your adult relationships? If it wasn't your parents, perhaps you learned it from a teacher, coach, a friend's parent, a neighbor, relative, or someone else like a long-time boyfriend. What did you see, hear, and experience?

I Saw:

_____

_____

_____

_____

_____

I Heard:

_____

_____

_____

_____

I Experienced:

_____

_____

_____

_____

_____

QUESTION 2

How did you cope or respond to what you saw, heard, and experienced? Notice how it's related to your Sore Spot. Did you get tough? Did you become a victim? Did you fight back or go into a shell? Did you decide that you didn't need anyone to care about you? What did you begin to do to avoid or cope with what your parent(s) did? Remember, you did the best you could at the time. Your response worked for you then. Remember, too, that we're not blaming here or digging up old negative feelings. Your parents were doing the best they knew how based on what they learned from their parents. How did you cope/respond to what you saw, heard, and experienced?

Examples:
I became shy and avoided social events like Girl Scouts,
dances, roller-skating.
I tried to do everything perfectly.
I cried until I got my way.
I withdrew and avoided them.

_____

_____

_____

_____

_____

_____

17

The Things We Do
For Love

*"Do not confine your children to your learning
for they were born in another time."*
CHINESE PROVERB

We know how what our parents said and did contributed to
the Sore Spot, but what role did we play in all this? It all
depends on what we had to do to feel in control and get
attention from our parents. When we behaved a certain way,
like whining, and when we received attention from that
behavior, we kept whining until it became a conditioned
behavior. We learned we could control how much attention
we received by how much we whined. So, how do you get a
sense of control and attention? Are you a Chaser? Joker?
Guilter? Saver? Fire Starter?

The following are examples of Destructive habits or
behaviors that come from what you experienced as a child.
You may see bits of yourself in one or more of these. It's
okay. You're not alone. Remember, for the most part all of
the behaviors listed below are either out of conscious
awareness or we blame our partner for making us act that
way. For instance, your partner may be passive while you are

dominating and controlling, but you shrug it off saying, "I wouldn't have to control everything if he would just make a decision once in a while." Sometimes we're so close to the problem that we can't see it for what it really is.

1. **THE CHASER:** Linda seeks approval by putting more into the relationship than Barry does. She is a Chaser and thinks Barry is better than her, so she's constantly trying to please him. Linda is attracted to men who aren't attracted to her and she's not interested in anyone who is interested in her. This is very safe for her because she doesn't have to risk getting close to anyone, since they don't want her anyway. By chasing what she can't have, she avoids letting anyone get to know the real her, believing that if they did, they wouldn't like what they saw and would eventually leave her. Linda complains to her friends and family that she can't find a good guy. Or her friends might scold her for always going after the wrong guys. Either way she's getting attention for behaving this way. As a child, Linda didn't get the approval she needed from her parents. By not getting approval, she felt she wasn't worthy. So she began to seek their approval by proving her worth. Now, when Barry rejects her or pulls away, Linda feels the need to prove him wrong. The more he rejects her, the more she tries to prove him wrong, causing him to pull away even more. Many times a Chaser feels that she alone is not enough. So she gives sex to men in hopes that they will find her to be worthy. She is confusing sex with love and more and more she feels less worthy and less lovable.

2. **THE AMBUSHER:** Karen launches preemptive strikes against the men she dates. As a child, she felt abandoned by her parents. Now, as an adult, she sabotages the relationship and does things to hurt him. Her attitude is, "I'll hurt you before you can hurt me."

3. **THE JUMPER:** Mandy jumps into relationships and commits quickly because she fears the longer she goes without commitment, the better the chance he discovers the real her and, she believes, he won't want the real her. She thinks, "If he gets to know the real me, I'm afraid he won't stick around." Or, instead of rushing to commitment, she may do the opposite and avoid commitment at any cost. As a Jumper, Mandy attracts men who jump in just as quickly or do the opposite and run away. When he leaves, her fears are reinforced and she says, "I knew it!" This only makes her jump in faster the next time.

4. **THE AVOIDER:** Jenny avoids intimacy. She thinks, "Why bother getting so intimate since he's eventually going to leave anyway?" Jenny doesn't share intimacies with her boyfriend, Kieren, due to her fear of rejection and abandonment. Deep down Jenny believes, "Right now he thinks I'm worthy, but I'm not. When he discovers the real me he won't want me anymore." Jenny's parents rejected her when she was a child. A parent can abandon a child even if they're still physically present. For some people a devastating break-up in the past, along with the memory of the pain of his leaving, causes them to avoid the risk of loving again.

5. **THE MANIPULATOR:** Heather uses emotions to drop hints or send signals to get what she wants. At the same time, she feels aggravated if Greg doesn't figure out what she wants. She says things like, "He should just know what I need," "He should have known to call me," "He should know how much I wanted to go" and "He should be able to figure out what I want on his own." Heather thinks if she acts moody Greg will ask, "What's wrong?" But when he does, she says, "Nothing." Greg can't read her mind and eventually he'll stop asking.

6. **THE GIVER:** As a child, Dana felt neglected and unloved. Because of this she developed an insatiable thirst for love and attention. As an adult, Dana overwhelms Rick with love and attention with the hope that he will treat her in kind. This comes from her fear of abandonment. The fear causes her to give and give so that he won't leave her. "If I give to him more and more, then he will find me more worthy and he won't want to leave me." Dana sometimes does things for Rick even though she doesn't want to. She also depends on Rick to make her happy, thinking, "If he would just pay more attention to me, I would be happy." Dana accepts being belittled by Rick because deep inside she believes he is better than her. She often apologizes even though it wasn't her fault. Dana gives and gives because she believes alone she is not enough. Dana ignores or denies her own needs and desires. She believes she is being unselfish when in reality she is being self-neglectful. As a Giver, Dana is constantly hoping Rick will notice how much she sacrifices and suffers. But that doesn't happen.

7. **THE TAKER:** As a Taker, Jaime criticizes and punishes her partner, BJ. She takes, takes, takes, but never gives anything in return. She criticizes his family, friends, career, and anything else that he's associated with. She always has to be right and everything has to be done her way. Jaime ignores or embarrasses BJ and treats him like a child by yelling things like, "You don't know anything. Why do you even open your mouth?" and, "Who taught you how to dress?" She never asks nicely, but instead demands forcefully. If she's not getting her way, Jaime withholds love and attention until she does. When she's not yelling she's being sarcastic or condescending, calling him names like moron and booby prize. These are all forms of punishment and she thinks by punishing him he'll change. He won't. What's more, as a Taker, Jaime feels guilty for punishing Rick, but at the same time resents him for her guilty feelings. So she begins

punishing him all over again. The real reason Jaime criticizes Rick is to keep him at a distance. Her subconscious rationale is, "If I keep him far enough away, he won't discover that I'm really not worthy." So she hides her insecurities behind a wall of control and criticism.

8. **THE WITHOLDER:** Emily watched her mother give and give and give to her father and never receive anything in return. So Emily became the opposite of her mother. She believes a woman who gives to her husband will have to continue giving more and more thus causing her to not want to give at all. So she withholds her love and attention, which makes her feel in control and more worthy, and therefore more lovable.

9. **THE GUILTER:** Danielle controls Jess by using guilt. As a child, she learned that making her parents feel guilty was the best way to be in control and to get attention. She would say things like, "You don't really love me" or "If you really love me you won't go on your trip." Notice how these words translate to adulthood. Do you know anyone who says or does things to guilt their partner into doing things their way or giving them what they want? Danielle gets attention and feels in control by using guilt to manipulate Jess. This makes her feel more worthy and lovable.

10. **THE SAVER:** Billie's mother was abusive toward her father, who never fought back. Subconsciously, Billie empathized with her father and chose to prove to the men in her life that women can be trusted, loving, and sweet. So, she dates men who need fixing or saving. The problem is, the men who need saving take advantage of her. She gives to Steve in order to prove her worth to him. She thinks, "If I'm there for him he'll be there for me, so I'd better give him whatever he needs." But he's never there for her. He's a Taker. Why should he give

anything in return when he's getting it all without lifting a finger? Billie is trying to save Steve by solving his problems for him. She thinks, "I know what's best for Steve" and, "Because I'm so generous, that means I'm worthy of being loved." By saving the men in her life, Billie is really controlling them. Also, by staying busy saving her partner she avoids dealing with her own problems, so she avoids failing at her own goals and dreams. Billie continues Saving Steve even when it's not good for her. She pays his rent and car payment even though she's barely able to pay her own. By thinking she's saving him, she gets attention, which makes her feel more worthy and lovable.

"A torn jacket is soon mended,
but hard words bruise the heart of a child."
HENRY WADSWORTH LONGFELLOW

11. **THE FIRESTARTER:** Lyndsay creates little bonfires in her life. She goes from crisis to crisis and expects Duane to save her. Lyndsay does this because her father was never there for her as a child. So she constantly tests Duane to make sure he'll be there when she needs him. But starting little fires and waiting to be rescued makes Duane lose respect for Lyndsay and he begins to resent her. By starting fires, Lyndsay gets attention and feels in control and these, as we know, make her feel more worthy and loved.

12. **THE SPOILED PRINCESS:** Erin acts like a child to get power, sympathy, and to avoid any responsibility. Pouting, sulking, ignoring, throwing tantrums, and storming away are her child-like behaviors. Acting like a child in the past has given Erin what she's wanted. In response to her tantrums, her boyfriend, Tim, asks what's wrong or apologizes and begs forgiveness. This gives her

attention and a sense of control. Everyone walks on eggshells around her waiting and not knowing when or what will set off another tantrum. By keeping them off-balance she is in control. Another reason for acting this way may be to avoid intimacy. If Erin fears commitment or wants to avoid real issues in the relationship, she may blow up at something else. This causes Tim to leave her alone and gets her out of a sticky situation. The problem is the issue never gets resolved and the Destructive behavior continues.

13. **THE VICTIM:** Bailey blames Joel for any problems in the relationship. She says things like, "I'm not overreacting, you just don't understand," or "I'm not jealous, you just don't love me enough." As the Victim, Bailey blames everyone and everything else and never takes responsibility herself. Everything happens *to* her and it's never her fault.

14. **THE EQUALIZER:** Kathleen gets even by "giving back" everything Justin "dishes out." She usually does this when her feelings have been hurt. Kathleen believes in the old adage, "An eye for an eye." If he hurt her, then she has to hurt him back. Sometimes she hurts him and he doesn't even know he hurt her. This is how Danielle thinks she can change him. Hurting him back makes her feel superior and more worthy. In the end, all it really does is slowly erode any love there was between them until there is only anxiety and resentment.

15. **THE ENTERTAINER:** When Susan doesn't know how to deal with a situation and feels uncomfortable, she tells jokes or acts like it's no big deal. But deep inside she's hurting and wishing someone would give her love and attention for being herself, rather than for being the life of the party. When someone complements her, she makes a joke about it rather than saying, "Thank you." She believes if she makes light of the situation she'll get the

love and attention she needs. But notice how she's ignoring the attention she's already getting. By being entertaining, Susan believes people will find her to be more worthy and lovable. She won't let them see the real Susan. This way she can avoid dealing with what's uncomfortable, unfamiliar, and unpredictable.

16. **THE SUPPRESSOR:** As a child, Darcy was taught to avoid conflict at any cost. She was told it's inappropriate to express her anger and frustration. This created resentment because she ignored her true feelings and never resolved her issues. Her pent up frustration causes Darcy to explode or storm away when she feels an overwhelming loss of control and attention. This makes her feel even less worthy and reinforces her belief that she shouldn't express her anger. Suppressing her feelings makes her feel more worthy, but at what price? By ignoring her husbands' insults, she is giving him the message that she's okay with it and he can go on insulting her. Darcy also rationalizes his Destructive behavior as a way to avoid conflict. She says, "Look at all that he provides for me, why should I complain?" But she's really just chipping away at her self-worth.

17. **THE PERFECTIONIST:** Molly learned she always had to do more to get love, attention, acceptance, and approval from her parents. She learned whatever she did was not enough. Now, she always has to do more to get the attention of her husband, Don. Her parents were perfectionists and extreme disciplinarians. So, she learned early on how to create excuses for mistakes or failures. By making excuses, she covered up her fear of not being good enough and not being lovable. Blaming someone or something else takes the attention off of her and makes her feel more worthy.

18. **THE COMPETITOR:** Cheryl had to fight to get anything in her family and she learned early on how to be

a competitor. In her relationships she feels she has to be smarter, tougher, and better at everything than her boyfriend, Randy. By being better than him she never has to depend on him. For Cheryl, depending on Randy is a sign of weakness. This keeps her from getting too close to him, but also keeps her feeling alone and isolated. She gets frustrated that she can't find the "right" guy when the truth is, she may already have met him. She just couldn't recognize him because she never lets herself get too close. Competing and winning makes her feel superior and more worthy, and ultimately, more lovable.

These are the primary styles. You may find yourself in one or more of these styles and to varying degrees. What I want you to notice is how each one of these types can be whittled down to feeling unworthy and what we do to compensate for it. Notice how each type attempts to gain a sense of control and tries to get attention by acting a certain way. When we have a sense of control and we're getting attention, we feel more worthy and more lovable. So we control or give up control, compete, give, take, or try to be perfect all so we can feel more worthy.

When we get attention and have a sense of control we feel more worthy.

But notice, also, that this comes from emotional thinking and is only short-term and transparent. Since it is only short-term, we must behave this way more frequently in order to feel more worthy more often. We need more attention and control in order to feel more worthy. It's similar to the alcoholic who always needs more liquor to feel good. Logical thinking won't help solve the problem.

Each of us needs attention and to feel in control of our world and of ourselves. Ask yourself, "How is what I'm doing and saying aimed at getting me attention and control? How is it aimed at making me feel worthy and loved?" Let's look at a few more examples of attention-getting behaviors.

BITTERSWEET ATTENTION

In the movie, *Charlie and the Chocolate Factory,* the main characters all utilize different means for getting attention. Veruca Salt is a demanding Spoiled Princess. She gets attention and a sense of control by making demands and holding her parents hostage, so to speak. Her father gets attention by giving in to her demands and being the "provider." Violet Beauregarde's attention getting behavior is being a Competitor. Her mother is an Idealist who gets attention by bragging about her daughters' trophies. She also feels more worthy by living her lost childhood through Violets' childhood.

Tommy TeaVee is a Dictator who gets attention and control by being an aggressive know-it-all. His father gets attention and control by playing the victim and lamenting his son's aggressive, uncontrollable nature. Agustus Gloop is a Taker who overeats to get attention and control. By being greedy and infantile, he feels more worthy. His mother feels better about herself by pampering Agustus and feeding him to appease him. She gets attention and feels in control by being a mom. In a way, she's symbolically still breast feeding him and keeping him a child longer so she doesn't have to give up her identity of "mother." Charlie Bucket is a Giver. He continually puts others ahead of himself and this gives him attention and a sense of control. His grandfather is a Taker who plays the Victim by lying in bed lamenting his layoff from the chocolate factory. He also demands that it be he who accompanies Charlie to the factory.

Finally, Willy Wonka acts like a child to get attention. Wonka is more of a combination of the Avoider, Chaser, Perfectionist, and Giver. He avoids letting anyone get too close to him but longs to be loved at the same time. He throws his perfectionist energies into his candies. He wants desperately to have a sense of control and get attention for who he truly is so he can feel more worthy and lovable. His father is a Dictator who feels more worthy and lovable by having complete control over his son.

We all do certain things to get attention. It is normal to want attention and to feel in control of our lives. It doesn't mean you're selfish or a bad person. We all do things to make ourselves feel better. When we feel better about ourselves we feel more loved. The problem is if you believe you have to behave Destructively in order to receive attention and feel in control, it's a Sore Spot.

When we feel better about ourselves we feel more loved.

CARRIE & JONATHAN

Jonathan is a Saver, while his wife Carrie is a Firestarter. She creates crises in the relationship and her life, but subconsciously she never wants to resolve them. If she puts out the fire she won't get the attention she craves. And what would happen if she attempts to resolve a crisis and discovers she cannot? She'll feel less worthy. So Carrie avoids trying to resolve the crises in order to feel more worthy and lovable. Consciously, she may think she is doing something to stamp out the fires. Or she may believe she's not capable and needs someone to sweep in and save the day. She starts the fires and then walks away from them.

Jonathan likes to save Carrie from her crises. He feels more worthy when he's able to solve her problems. But because he can't get her to talk about any crises she complains about, he's unable to fix things. As a result, he feels less worthy and less lovable. If she talks about her issues they might get resolved and then where would she get attention? She'd have to create more crises. If Jonathan solves all her problems, he'd have nothing to make himself feel better. Luckily Carrie isn't going to stop starting fires, so Jonathan will always have enough fuel to feed his self-worth. Carrie feels less worthy because Jonathan isn't saving her, even though she's thwarting all his efforts. Jonathan feels he's not good enough because he can't save her. And round and round they go.

As human beings we sometimes work in opposites. If I feel weak, I act overly strong. If I feel stupid, I act like I know everything. If I fear commitment, I scare you away so you won't want to commit. If I don't like myself, I hate and put down others. What are you doing that is the opposite of how you really feel?

Complete the following exercise being totally honest with yourself and seeing through the rationalizations and excuses you normally use to explain your behavior.

I ACT THIS WAY...　　　**BUT I REALLY FEEL...**

Example:
I act high and mighty...but I really feel insecure.

I ACT THIS WAY...　　　**BUT I REALLY FEEL...**

_____

_____

_____

_____

_____

18

The Blame Game

"He that is good for making excuses is seldom good for anything else."

BENJAMIN FRANKLIN

Would you sit in the passenger seat of your dream car if there was no one behind the wheel, it was going down a steep hill, and you knew it had no brakes? Yet that is exactly what some people do in their relationships. They become a passenger in their relationship and expect it to just take them to "happily ever after." When it doesn't, they actually blame the car for crashing. They ignore the red flags in the beginning and then blame their partner for their eventual unhappiness. They say, "If only he did this or if only he didn't do that, then I'd finally be happy." Ultimately, we cannot control our partner; at least not for very long. We can only control ourselves. It's time you get behind the wheel instead of letting your partner, or worse, your Sore Spot drive the relationship.

By getting behind the wheel you take charge of where your relationship is headed. But even though you're behind the wheel you still have control over only *three* things in your life:

1. What You **Think**

2. What you **Feel**

3. What You **Do**

By taking charge of these three things you control the quality of your relationship. Notice these are the first three elements on the Mental Merry-Go-Round. You may also notice that you cannot control what anyone else thinks, feels, or does.

WHAT YOU THINK

Obviously you can't control what someone else is thinking and no one can control what you think about. The thoughts in your mind are generated by you and for you. Parents, teachers, boyfriends, the media, celebrities, and friends can all influence our thoughts but it is still your choice as to what thoughts occupy your mind. Our thoughts are influenced by others when our values are similar or in opposition to theirs.

VALUES

Values are what make us do the things we do, and they are what we use to evaluate what we've done or how we've behaved. If I have an affair and feel guilty about it, I have violated one of my values. If I don't feel guilty about it that means fidelity is not a value I hold dear to myself. In short, our values are what are important to us. Obviously I'm going to spend more time thinking about what's important to me than what's not important. I'm also going to spend more time thinking about what's important to me than what's important to you.

Growing up you observe, accept, and internalize some of your parents' values. For example, your parents may value a strong, close-knit family. If you agree and accept this value as your own, then you will seek a relationship that will become a loving, happy family. You have to first agree with your parents' value in order to accept it as your own. From that point forward, your thoughts will be in line with that value. Your thoughts won't be about dating as many men as you can before you turn thirty. Instead, your thoughts will be focused on finding a guy who has the same values as you, settling down with him, and starting a family.

Of course you could rebel against your parents' values in which case your thoughts will be in opposition to their values. Either way your parents do not make you think anything. Your decision to accept or avoid any of their values will cause you to think certain thoughts pertaining to that choice. This is how others, like our parents, influence our thoughts. In the end, though, you alone are in charge of your thoughts.

"Everybody has pain; suffering is optional."
DALAI LAMA

WHAT YOU FEEL

No one can make you angry. Instead, you choose to be angry. Likewise, you can't make anyone happy; you can only make yourself happy. You cannot make me happy. I'm happier when I'm with you and that is entirely up to me. You cannot make me feel anything. It is up to me to choose to feel a particular feeling. That choice is the thought that leads to the feeling. Your mind makes that choice by comparing the current situation with similar past experiences.

You cannot make me happy.
I'm happier when I'm with you,

For instance, when I'm an hour late for our lunch date, your mind begins searching for similar past experiences to compare it with so it can determine how to react. If there is no similar experience in your past, your mind will search for how your parents behaved in similar situations. When, in a split second, it finds the memory of being stood up on prom night, you'll equate the two and become sad or angry. If it uncovers a memory of a friend who missed a lunch with you because he was in a terrible accident, your mind will compare the two events and cause you to feel anxious or worried. This is where our minds begin to race if we're not careful. We can prevent this by becoming aware of what we're thinking and taking control of those thoughts.

If I show up an hour late for our date, there is only one thing that is true; I am an hour late. It is entirely up to you to feel worried, angry, sad, frustrated, ambivalent, anxious, calm, disappointed, or overjoyed. None of those emotions is going to change the fact that I am an hour late. It is you who has complete control over your thoughts. When the thought pops into your head, it is completely in your control to change it. There is nobody saying you have to repeatedly think I'm a jerk for being an hour late. You control your thoughts, and therefore you control how you feel.

If I show up an hour late for our date
there is only one thing that is true;
I am an hour late.

WHAT YOU DO

Finally, no one can make you do anything. Even if they're holding a gun to your head, it is still your decision to do what he says or take a chance that he won't pull the trigger. Likewise, you can't control how someone else behaves. For instance, you can't make someone stop yelling at you. He must choose to stop yelling. It is always a choice to hit another person or call them names. Abuse is a choice just like buying a car is a choice. What we do is determined by the thought that precedes the behavior. When you're angry, it is you who chooses to respond in anger.

Mahatma Gandhi was angry with the British but instead of lashing out in anger, he chose to respond with love. By doing so, he was able to bring to an end the British occupation of India. If he had responded with anger, there would have been bloodshed and many lives lost. Because he responded with peace and love, India was eventually given its independence and not a single life was lost.

"A man may fall many times but he won't be a failure until he says someone pushed him."

ELMER G. LETTERMAN

What you tell yourself about the situation and how it compares to past similar events, or in other words, your thoughts, are what make you angry. Everything begins with a thought and trickles down from there. When you understand this process, your relationship changes and you begin to enjoy your ride on the Mental Merry-Go-Round.

VICTIM THINKING vs. REALITY THINKING

There's a big difference between Victim thinking and Reality thinking. Victim thinking feeds the unpleasant feelings and behaviors, while Reality thinking keeps things in perspective and keeps you more calm and centered.

Victim Thinking	Reality Thinking
That bastard blew me off!	*He didn't call me.*
What an annoying habit.	*He's eating his peas one at a time.*
He's driving me crazy!	*He sure has a lot of energy tonight.*

Playing the victim fills our need to feel worthy by feeling more important while making someone or something else seem less important. This makes us feel superior, which gives a false boost to our self-esteem. When we label the experience as wrong or bad, it makes us resent the other person or situation. Resentment is an emotion that slowly eats away at us from the inside out. Holding on to resentment is like taking poison and waiting for the *other* person to die. How much sense does that make?

Harboring resentment is like taking poison and waiting for the other person to die.

You've seen two people respond differently to the same situation. One gets angry, the other laughs and walks away. One says, "He cheated on me so I can never trust another man again" while another says, "*Because* he cheated, I learned a lot about myself and a lot about what I really want in my ideal partner." It's the choice that makes us respond one way or another, not the situation. If it were the situation we'd all respond the same way.

We all know people who play the victim to everything that happens in their relationships. They usually point their finger and blame something or someone else for everything bad that happens in their relationships.

BLAME

Most people who aren't happy in their relationship will blame their partner, the dating service, the city in which they live, their parents, friends, or the fact they have no money. They say things like, "My marriage would have worked if he'd only paid more attention to me" and, "I could have a great relationship if only I didn't work so much." Blaming someone or something else only gives away your power. If you give away your power, you cannot change it. Blaming someone

220

else for your situation will only deprive you of the power to do anything about it. Until you change, nothing will.

Blaming someone else for your situation will only deprive you of the power to do anything about it.

The victim thinks there's something wrong with *him*. He did this or he doesn't do that. But you can't control what someone thinks, feels, or does. You can only control what you think, feel, and do. It is only by changing *your* behavior that you can change his. This makes sense because when you change what you are doing, he has to change what he's doing or leave the relationship. If you change what you are doing, then what he's doing no longer works.

If someone is yelling at you and you peacefully say you're not going to discuss anything until he calms down, is he going to keep yelling? Would you be able to keep yelling at someone if they remained completely calm and unnerved? Change what you're doing and he'll change what he's doing. Stop blaming everyone and everything and start taking charge of your relationship. No one else can do it for you.

JUSTIFY

The other way people play the victim is by justifying or rationalizing their actions. They may say, "I don't have time" but we both know if you want it bad enough you'll make the time. We've all been so busy at work that we don't even have thirty seconds to eat our lunch. Yet we manage to find a minute to call and get our sweetie fix, don't we? If it's important you'll find the time.

Others use justifications like, "I don't have enough money to take someone out on a date." If you want it bad enough you'll find the money. Whether it's a stereo, new wardrobe, or a weekend at the spa, we somehow manage to find the money for it. If it's important, you'll either find the money or find an inexpensive way to take him out.

Another popular justification is, "I'm too old" or "I'm too young." Colonel Sanders was sixty-five years old when he started Kentucky Fried Chicken. Mozart was five years old when he started composing and was published at the ripe old age of seven. You're never too young or too old for anything, so stop using it as an excuse.

You are the one person who is always present in all your relationships.

You are the one person who is always present in all your relationships. That means the Sore Spots that keep popping up don't have anything to do with him and everything to do with you. That's not to blame you or make you feel bad. It's simply to point out that you are in charge of the quality of your relationship, and until you change, nothing will. Instead of thinking there's something wrong with him or he did this or he didn't do that, we should be focused on what *we* can do differently.

You can't control or change someone else. You can only control what *you* think and what *you* do. People who play the victim blame other people or events for their problems. If we blame someone or something else for our Sore Spot, then we have to change *them.* As you well know, you cannot change anyone. You can only change yourself. To paraphrase Gandhi, you must be the change you want to see in your relationship.

"There are two primary choices in life: to accept conditions as they exist or accept the responsibility for changing them."
DENIS WAITLEY

When you accept that you are in charge of all of your thoughts, feelings, and behaviors, you become empowered and capable of making dramatic changes. Those who believe that stuff happens to them and they are powerless to do anything about it will wander aimlessly through their relationship playing the role of victim, blaming their partner, and making excuses for their unhappiness. Those who play the role of victim in their relationships are like corks floating in a stream. They believe they are powerless against the tides, winds, and currents.

Those who take charge of the quality of their relationships are the ones who fasten a rudder and a sail to their cork and take control of the direction in which they sail. You are in charge of your thoughts, feelings, and behaviors. There is no one making you do anything. This is great news because it means that if you don't like a certain result in your life, you have the power to change it. By taking charge of your thoughts, feelings, and behaviors you start getting the results you want.

"Be the change you want to see in the world."
MAHATMA GANDHI

WHO'S IN CHARGE HERE?

Let's play a game. Think about your past and current relationships and deny any responsibility for them. Really focus on how everything in your relationships is a result of random things happening and other people doing things to you. Completely deny any responsibility at all for your relationships, past and present. You are a victim of circumstances. It wasn't your fault.

Now, change your focus and accept complete responsibility for your thoughts, feelings, and behaviors. Accept total responsibility for your relationships. Everything that has happened in your relationships is the result of the sum total of all your thoughts, decisions, beliefs, feelings, and actions from the time you were born until now. Notice how empowered you feel when you accept responsibility. Responsibility does not mean blame. It simply means you are in charge of your thoughts, feelings, and behavior and, ultimately, the results you get.

When you are in charge of your relationship, you are solution thinking. If you are playing the victim of your relationship, you are problem thinking. Which do you think is more empowering? The difference between being a victim and taking responsibility is the difference between being actively involved in your relationship or just passively accepting whatever happens to you.

"It's not our abilities that show what we truly are.
It is our choices."

ALBUS DUMBLEDORE
HARRY POTTER AND THE CHAMBER OF SECRETS

Responsibility and blame do not mean the same thing. When someone places blame, they are finding fault with that person or situation. Responsibility is making a decision. If you don't make your own decisions, someone else will be making them for you. Responsibility is ownership. When you own something, you have power over it. I'm not saying you're to blame for all the bad stuff that happens. I am saying you are in charge of how you respond when bad stuff happens. How you respond to bad things and the choices you make determine the success of your relationships. When bad stuff happens, do you slip into problem thinking or solution thinking? Things don't always go as planned, so how you respond determines the quality of your relationships. As a child, if you were mistreated, it was not your fault. It will be your fault if you don't learn what you need to in order to break the cycle. And it's not too late.

If you don't make your own decisions,
someone else will make them for you.

BETHANY

Between the ages of twelve and fifteen, Bethany was sexually abused by her stepfather. Through counseling she was able to overcome the trauma and today is a rape victim counselor. Rather than play the victim, she took charge of what happened in her life and used it to help others overcome similar obstacles. Bethany also put together a rape prevention program that has helped keep thousands of women safe across the United States. She could have played the victim and felt sorry for herself but, instead, she chose to empower herself and others by educating other women on how to prevent sexual abuse. Bethany attached a rather large sail to her cork and took charge of which direction she travels.

We all need consistent and healthy love and attention from our parents if we are to give and receive love and attention constructively as adults. Growing up, my father showed more love to his dogs than he did to me. He gave more attention to his car and TV than he did to me. What does a child learn from this? He learns that he doesn't matter, that he's invisible, that he's not worthy of being loved. At a subconscious level I was thinking to myself, "Dad hates me. He's going to hit me and yell at me today and there's nothing I can do about it. I know he wishes I didn't exist. I just want him to love me. What did I do wrong?" This left me feeling powerless and helpless.

I tell you this not because I want you to feel sorry for me. I tell you this because I want you to know you can overcome it. If I can do it, anyone can. As a child, my options were limited. As an adult, your options are unlimited and it is up to you to resolve your past and regain your personal power and control over it.

If I fail to do so as an adult, I doom myself to miserable relationships. It's like a bird in Alaska who doesn't fly south for the winter. Instead he stays in Alaska and endures snow, ice, wind, and sub-zero temperatures. Rather than learning from his

225

previous chilly experiences, he stays behind hoping this winter it will be sunny and warm. But each winter he freezes and barely makes it through to spring. Consequently, he may come to believe relationships are hard and aren't meant to be pleasant or fulfilling. I chose to learn from my past and change the quality of my relationships. As a result, my relationships are exciting, fulfilling, and rewarding. Challenges still come up but they don't dredge up my past like they used to.

Most of us demand from our partners what we didn't get from our parents.

Remember, through your thoughts you create everything and everyone that is and is not in your life. Every thought, feeling, and behavior has led you to whatever relationship situation you are in right now. If you want to change your situation, you have to change what you think, what you feel, and what you do. You can't change someone else; you can only change you.

Most of us demand from our partners what we didn't get from our parents. We expect our partner to make our unpleasant childhood memories go away. When he can't do that, we may leave and look for someone else who can fix us. The only person who can fix you is you. The first step is acknowledging that you are in command of what you think, what you feel, and what you do. By taking charge of these three things, you control the quality of your relationships.

"There is little difference in people, but that little difference makes a big difference. The little difference is attitude. The big difference is whether it is positive or negative."

W. CLEMENT STONE

QUESTION 1

How have you played the role of victim in your relationships? Make a list of the things you do, say, and think that put the blame on your partner. Be honest. We all do it from time to time. So what do you do, say, and think that makes him wrong and you right?

Example:
I PLAY THE VICTIM BY: I nag him to load the dishwasher the "right" way.

THE REALITY IS: One person's right may be another person's wrong. He loads it the way his family did growing up. The dishes still get clean whether the spoons are placed handle up or handle down. At least he loads the dishwasher.

I PLAY THE VICTIM BY: I think to myself what a jerk he is for not being more romantic. I think that if he really loved me he would be more like the kind of guy I want him to be. This makes me more frustrated and I begin to resent him more.

THE REALITY IS: He is who he is. I knew this going into the relationship. While he's not very romantic, he does go along with my romantic plans and he never complains. I guess he is romantic in his own way. Just because I have a different idea of what romance is doesn't mean it's the only way to be romantic.

I PLAY THE VICTIM BY:

_____

_____

_____

_____

_____

_____

THE REALITY IS:

_____

_____

_____

_____

_____

I PLAY THE VICTIM BY:

_____

_____

_____

_____

_____

_____

THE REALITY IS:

_____

_____

_____

_____

_____

_____

I PLAY THE VICTIM BY:

_____

_____

_____

_____

_____

THE REALITY IS:

_____

_____

_____

_____

_____

_____

19

Making Your Past History

"Those who do not remember the past are condemned to repeat it."

GEORGE SANTAYANA

LOVE'S LESSONS

If we can find meaning in the experiences that made us feel meaningless we can accelerate the healing of a Sore Spot. So it's crucial that we learn today the lessons from yesterday. When people grieve, they get comfort knowing that the loss has meaning. If there is no meaning, the grief is more severe and longer lasting. In fact, when we find meaning from a painful event it gives our immune system a boost while simultaneously reducing our feelings of anxiety and sadness. Learning from an event and noticing what benefits we received from the experience actually help us live longer, healthier lives. We discovered the silver lining from our Sore Spot back in chapter six. Now it's time to uncover the meaning.

Have you ever done something that didn't turn out the way you wanted and you thought, "Wow. I really learned my lesson?" When we 'learn our lesson,' we don't make the same mistake again. If we look back on the Sore Spot, we will notice that we didn't learn our lesson when we first had the opportunity. If we did, there wouldn't be a Sore Spot.

By now you're aware that these lessons repeat themselves until we learn them. You will date the same kind of guys, be controlling in the same situations, run from commitment each time he gets too close, or repeatedly run the same pattern over and over until you learn what you were supposed to learn the first time. The good news is it's never too late to go back and learn our lesson. That is what this step is all about.

When you lose, don't lose the lesson.

The best lessons are always:

1. **Positive**
2. About **yourself**
3. About the **future**

If the lesson is negative, about someone else, and stated in past tense, you will not experience growth and understanding and you will not change your Destructive approach. For instance, if you say, "It wasn't my fault. He was wrong for doing that to me," this lesson is negative (*it wasn't*), it is about someone else (*he*), and it is set in the past (*wasn't, was wrong).* The lesson should be rephrased to be most effective.

"Tough times don't last. Tough people do."
COACH PAUL "BEAR" BRYANT

The rephrased lesson could be, "I'm going to stick up for myself next time." This lesson is definitely positively stated, it is only for you, and it is stated in future tense (*next time*). This is a perfect lesson. With this lesson, you are able to make more appropriate decisions that will more effectively fulfill your needs. When looking back, you are able to discover new lessons that were overlooked at the time. By learning these lessons, we're able to change the decision that was made at the time and make a healthier, more appropriate decision in its place. You don't have to forget your past; you just need to learn from it so you don't make the same mistake again. It's important to understand that you were doing the best you knew how at the time. But now you know better.

> *You don't have to forget your past.*
> *You just need to learn from it so you*
> *don't make the same mistake again.*

In the movie, *Eternal Sunshine of the Spotless Mind,* after Joel and Clementine break-up they have their memories of each other erased so they can avoid the pain attached to those memories. However, they continue to meet and start a relationship and eventually run into the same problems over and over. Why? When they erased the memories, they erased their lessons as well. Without the lessons, we are doomed to repeat the same mistakes over and over again.

The opposite is seen in the film, *Groundhog Day.* Phil Connors continually awakens and has to relive Groundhog Day until he learns what he's supposed to learn. In the beginning of this hellish cycle, he wants to give up and even attempts suicide. But once Phil decides to learn from his mistakes, his world takes on a whole new meaning and he is forever changed. The cycle ends and he lives the rest of his life a much happier man.

*"Good judgment comes from experience,
and a lot of that comes from bad judgment."*

WILL ROGERS

Let's look back at Kathleen's story and see how it could be different by learning her lessons. If you'll recall, Kathleen thought her husband, Gary, was cheating. She obsessed about the affair and imagined details that weren't really true. If we look at the Mental Merry-Go-Round we know that Kathleen could have changed her thoughts and been more aware of the facts. You get what you focus on and she could have focused on solution rather than problem. So, the first thing she could do differently next time is pay attention to the thoughts she's thinking and change her focus.

Second, she could take charge of her feelings and feel more empowered and confident. Her feelings reinforced her thoughts and vice versa. By feeling more resourceful emotions, she is able to respond more Constructively. Third, she could notice her pattern of Destructive behavior. Finally, she can go back to when the Sore Spot was created and become aware of how she was conditioned to behave that way. This allows her to change the behavior.

So she changes her focus and what she's thinking, she takes charge of how she feels, and she behaves Constructively. By taking these three steps, Kathleen has control over the quality of her relationship. She gets more of the results she wants and those results turn around and reinforce her thoughts. This let's her enjoy her ride on the Mental Merry-Go-Round. Since the facts proved Gary was not cheating, she would do better to dwell on the things she loves about him rather than her unfounded fear of infidelity.

"That which doesn't kill me makes me stronger."

FRIEDRICH NIETZSCHE

The next time you find yourself in a difficult or unpleasant situation, ask yourself one or all of the following questions:

1. What can I learn from this?
2. What can I do differently next time?
3. This being the case, how shall I proceed?

By asking yourself these questions, you put your mind in solution thinking mode. Furthermore, you attach meaning and value to the experience and you learn from it. This allows you to avoid repeating the same mistake in the future.

"A man is not old until regrets take the place of dreams."

PROVERB

QUESTION 1

Remember the first or earliest time your Sore Spot appeared. The most important memory to you when you know that's where it all began. Imagine sitting alone in a movie theater and watching that memory play on the screen like a movie. See yourself in the movie. Ask yourself, "What do I need to learn from this so that I can respond differently next time? What can I learn from this experience that will allow me to change the way I respond the next time something similar happens?" You may get one, ten, or fifty lessons but there is always at least one. As you receive these lessons, collect two or three, then open your eyes and write them down. Close your eyes and get more lessons. Once you're done getting the lessons, go back through the one's you listed and change any that need to be changed so that they are perfect lessons. Remember, lessons are Positive, about You, and Future oriented.

Examples:
Instead of blowing up I'm going to calmly talk about what's bothering me.
I'm going to enforce my boundaries next time.
I am brilliant to have learned all that I have on my own.
If I can do this, I can do anything.
I am limitless!
Everyone makes mistakes.
I can get attention by asking for it rather than having a tantrum.

Okay, it's your turn. What can you learn from this event that will allow you to respond Constructively next time?

_____

_____

_____

_____

_____

_____

_____

_____

_____

QUESTION 2

Recall your answer from question #4 in chapter six, that emotional need you satisfy from your reaction to the Sore Spot. Using the lessons you just received, what are some Constructive ways you could respond to similar situations in the future and still get that positive feeling next time? What can you do differently next time? Make a list.

Examples:
I can enforce my boundaries respectfully and tactfully.
I can share more of myself with people and it will improve my level of trust in them.
I can ask if we could sit down and discuss this problem so he will be more calm and willing to solve the problem.

_____

_____

_____

_____

_____

_____

_____

_____

_____

_____

SEEING THE FUTURE

Close your eyes. Imagine putting the unpleasant emotions from that Sore Spot into a rocket ship. Then launch the rocket into space and watch as it hurtles toward the sun. Finally, notice the rocket and those unpleasant feelings explode as it enters the sun.

From your seat in the theater, see that first or earliest memory on the screen once again. As you watch the movie of that memory, notice yourself responding Constructively where the Sore Spot used to be. Now notice how the other person in your memory responds. If there are any other people in the memory, notice how they respond. Notice how you feel as you witness the positive outcome for yourself and those around you. Start that memory from the beginning again and this time float into your body in the memory looking through your own eyes. Run that memory all the way through and make that Constructive choice again. What do you see? What do you hear? How do you feel? Really flood your body with those positive, empowering feelings.

Next, notice the movie fast forwarding to some time in the future. It may be this afternoon, tomorrow, next week, or next year. Notice the movie stop at some time in the future, in a relationship where something similar happens, and notice how you respond. Through your own eyes, notice yourself responding Constructively. Fill your body with the feelings associated with responding this way. Enjoy the moment for as long as you wish. When you're ready, come back to now and open your eyes.

Use this guided imagery for the next twenty-one days.

20

Happily Ever After?

"There will come a time when you
believe everything is finished.
That will be the beginning."

LOUIS L'AMOUR

Congratulations! You should now be more aware of how the Sore Spot was created and when and why it keeps popping up. Because of this awareness, you should be able to respond more Constructively the next time it does. You have begun rewiring those millions of nerve cells and strengthened the new connection a couple of times. In order to reinforce our new habit it is important to follow-up for twenty-one days using the *Sore Spot Pattern Interrupt* from chapter 15 and *Seeing The Future* from chapter 19. It may be easier to record the visualizations and listen to them every day. The more you do this, the more nerve cells you invite to the rewiring party and the sooner it becomes a habit. After a couple days you may find that you can no longer conjure up the image of that old Sore Spot. If this is the case, feel free to skip *Sore Spot Pattern Interrupt* and continue *Seeing The Future* for the full twenty-one days.

*"Coming together is a beginning,
staying together is progress,
and working together is success."*

HENRY FORD

FREEDOM OF CHOICE

Hold your right hand out. Make a fist. Now stick your thumb out. Your thumb represents the old behavior. Now open your hand and spread your fingers. Your four fingers represent other, more Constructive ways to respond in the future. Because we've been given the gift of free will, you will always have the option of choosing the thumb and responding the old way. It's not like that option disappears. However, you can now recognize it whenever it rears its ugly head and choose to respond in any of the more Constructive ways you've just discovered. The choices you make are the difference between having a happy, fulfilling relationship or a miserable, rotten relationship. You will always have to make a choice. Remember it all begins with a thought.

"First enlightenment, then the laundry."

BUDDHIST PROVERB

Do you know anyone who has tried to lose weight? That person will tell you it took time to put on the weight and it takes time to take the weight off. They'll admit you can't lose twenty pounds overnight. Sore Spots work the same way. It's not like switching a light on or off. Nothing works like that. It took a moment to make a decision and years to reinforce that decision. So it will take a little while to rewire your new decision. This is why you're *Seeing The Future* for twenty-one days. Just a couple minutes a day for twenty-one days will have you on the road to better relationships.

"I would rather regret the things that I have done than the things that I have not."

LUCILLE BALL

FANTASY OR REALITY

Recent studies have shown that visualizing yourself doing something stimulates the same muscles and nerve cells as if you were actually, physically doing it. In other words, the brain doesn't know the difference between fantasy and reality. This is important because what you believe to be real will be real.

Australian psychologist, Alan Richardson, conducted an experiment with basketball players. He took three groups of players and tested their ability to make free throws. Richardson instructed the first group to practice shooting free throws for twenty minutes each day. The second group was told to do nothing. The third group was asked to visualize themselves successfully making free throws for twenty minutes each day.

When he followed up, Richardson found that the group that did nothing had 0% improvement in free throw shooting. No surprise there. The first group improved by 24%. The third group, which only imagined successfully making free throws, improved by 23%. Did you get that? They improved almost as much as the group that actually shot free throws each day. This helps to explain why our heart races after imagining a first kiss or why our hands begin shaking just thinking about a frightening experience.

When you imagine yourself doing something, it rewires the nerve cells to respond as if you were actually, physically doing it. Research has shown that during guided imagery the muscles and nerves associated with the activity being imagined receive a tiny amount of stimulation. This stimulation is too minute for you to be aware of consciously. However, because the muscles are stimulated in the same way they would be if you actually performed the activity, your muscles remember how to react when the time actually comes. In other words, when you imagine yourself doing something, it creates a memory in those muscles and nerves of carrying out that activity *before* you even do it.

The only difference between mentally rehearsing and physically rehearsing is that you never have to make a mistake when mentally rehearsing. Everything you imagine can be perfect. As a result, your muscles and thoughts will remember to perform perfectly when the time comes. The more vivid and clear the mental images are, the more effective they will be. It may take some time to develop this skill. However, by practicing only five minutes a day, you will begin to notice measurable results in no time. Simply imagining something *is* a reality for your mind and your body.

> *"If you can dream it, you can do it.*
> *Always remember, this whole thing*
> *was started by a mouse."*
> WALT DISNEY

OUT WITH THE OLD AND IN WITH THE NEW

When you remove an old Destructive habit, you must replace it with a new Constructive habit or the old one will come back. The fact that you're now aware of the Sore Spot and what triggers it means you're capable of choosing how to respond. Every time you respond Constructively, you are reinforcing that behavior and making it harder to not respond that way. By being aware of your thoughts, you can change them. When you change your thought, you change your feelings and your behavior, and ultimately, the results you get. Those new results reinforce your new thoughts. And so it goes on the Mental Merry-Go-Round. After a bit of time and a number of repetitions, you will have reinforced your new habit to the point that the old habit isn't even an option any more.

Now that you've completed the program, you are looking at that former Sore Spot from a different point of view. This different perspective allows you to think differently about that Sore Spot. As you are well aware, now that your thoughts have changed, you will feel differently about it. As you feel better about it, you behave differently and more Constructively. Of course, behaving Constructively leads to more of the results you want.

"When someone loves you,
the way they say your name is different.
You know that your name is safe in their mouth."

BILLY - Age 4

Remember, it's going to rain on your parade from time to time. A tree experiences its greatest struggles in the spring just before it blooms. From rain comes beautiful flowers and abundant life. When it rains, you can hide inside and chant, "Rain, rain, go away, come again some other day." Or you can go outside and jump in the puddles. Splash around. Get wet. It's okay. You'll dry off.

If you're feeling impatient because things aren't happening as quickly as you had hoped, remember that big things take more time and energy to move. Once it gets moving, though, it will take bigger strides and create more momentum. The earth is always moving; yet, it's spinning so fast we cannot perceive ourselves as moving. Sometimes you just have to trust that, as imperceptible as it may be, you are indeed moving forward.

The point is you are going to experience the ebb and flow of your relationship from time to time. There are going to be low moments and there are going to be times when the world is your oyster. Remember, that each relationship is an opportunity to learn and grow. It is an opportunity to move forward.

> *"It's a little like wrestling a gorilla.*
> *You don't quit when you're tired,*
> *you quit when the gorilla is tired."*

ROBERT STRAUSS

Be the change you want to see in your relationship. Take control of your thoughts. Be in command of your feelings. Take charge of your behavior. Enjoy your ride on the Mental Merry-Go-Round. As you do, be aware of the envy others express as you begin to get more from your relationship. How will it feel when you fall in love all over again? How will it feel when you create a supportive and loving relationship? As you think, so you become.

Take charge of the Mental Merry-Go-Round and what you *think, feel,* and *do.* When you do, you will begin to Constructively attract the *attention* you need and feel a greater sense of *control.* This causes you to feel more *worthy* and ultimately makes you feel more *loved.*

It's up to you whether or not you enjoy your ride on the Mental Merry-Go-Round. Since there is no way to stop or get off the ride, you may as well enjoy it. Cinderella found out the hard way. She discovered the same things Snow White, Sleeping Beauty, and even Shrek came to understand: Happily Ever After depends on you and it starts with what you think, what you feel, and what you do.

> *"Flatter me, and I may not believe you.*
> *Criticize me, and I may not like you.*
> *Ignore me, and I may not forgive you.*
> *Encourage me, and I will not forget you."*

WILLIAM ARTHUR WARD

Please visit my website

www.scottkudia.com

*for free relationship reports and downloads,
audio seminars, and information regarding
upcoming events in your area.*

About the Author

As a bestselling co-author and through his popular seminars, Relationship Specialist, Scott Kudia, Ph.D., has empowered thousands to overcome their obstacles and experience a better love life. Scott's innovative work combines traditional psychology with the latest cutting edge technologies giving you the power to create more fulfilling relationships. His seminars are some of the most unique and powerful relationship events in the world. Scott's passionate and inspirational speaking style always leaves his audience enlightened, empowered, and thoroughly entertained. Above all, they leave with the ability to connect more deeply with their partner and ultimately get more from their relationships.

If you would like to set up an event with Scott, please email

info@scottkudia.com

Lightning Source UK Ltd.
Milton Keynes UK
UKOW06f2001171217
314641UK00015B/652/P